¡Canta Conmigo!

¡Canta Conmigo!

SONGS AND SINGING GAMES FROM GUATEMALA AND NICARAGUA

Rachel Gibson

Illustrations by
Patricia Sucely Puluc Tecúm

Oxford University Press is a department of the University of Oxford. It furthers
the University's objective of excellence in research, scholarship, and education
by publishing worldwide. Oxford is a registered trade mark of Oxford University
Press in the UK and certain other countries.

Published in the United States of America by Oxford University Press
198 Madison Avenue, New York, NY 10016, United States of America.

© Oxford University Press 2022

All rights reserved. No part of this publication may be reproduced, stored in
a retrieval system, or transmitted, in any form or by any means, without the
prior permission in writing of Oxford University Press, or as expressly permitted
by law, by license, or under terms agreed with the appropriate reproduction
rights organization. Inquiries concerning reproduction outside the scope of the
above should be sent to the Rights Department, Oxford University Press, at the
address above.

You must not circulate this work in any other form
and you must impose this same condition on any acquirer.

CIP data is on file at the Library of Congress
ISBN 978-0-19-753621-6

9 8 7 6 5 4 3 2 1

Printed by Marquis, Canada

For the teachers, children, and families who shared music for this book.

For Craig, Phoebe, and Levi. May we travel together always.

CONTENTS

Song Index • ix

Preface • xiii

Acknowledgments • xv

About the Companion Website • xvii

Part 1: Suggestions for Teachers and Context • 1
    Suggestions for Teachers • 3
    Living Traditions: Children's Music in Guatemala and Nicaragua • 7
    Overview: Central America, Guatemala, and Nicaragua • 9
    Fieldwork Locations • 13
    Biographies • 25

Part 2: La Música (The Music) • 37
    Rondas (Singing Games) • 39
    Rimas y Juegos (Rhymes and Games) • 69
    Canciones (Songs) • 93

Part 3: Beyond the Songs • 155
    Culturally Responsive and Sustaining Pedagogies • 157
    Music in Central America • 163
    A Brief History of Central America • 173

Appendix 1: Resources—Literature • 181

Appendix 2: Resources—Documentaries and Films • 183

Works Cited • 185

Bibliography • 187

Indexes • 191
    Sources: Sites and Singers • 191
    Subject • 195
    Song Type • 197
    Game and Movement Type • 199
    Formation • 201
    Notational Literacy • 203
    Spanish Language Learning • 205
    Alphabetical • 207

SONG INDEX

Rondas (Singing Games)

A pares y nones	(Evens and Odds)
Campanita de oro	(Little Gold Bell)
Doña Ana	(Doña Ana)
El caracolito	(The Little Snail)
El patio de mi casa (Guatemala)	(My Back Yard)
El patio de mi casa (Nicaragua)	(My Back Yard)
El toro toronjil	(The Toronjil Bull)
Juguemos en el bosque	(Let's Play in the Forest)
La pájara pinta (1)	(The Painted Bird)
La pájara pinta (2)	(The Painted Bird)
Nerón, Nerón	(Nerón, Nerón)
Pollos y pollitos	(Chickens and Chicks)
Que llueva	(Let It Rain)
Ronda de la mano	(Hand Circle Game)
Ronda el campanario	(Around the Bell Tower)
Rueda, rueda	(Around and Around)
Salí, tortuga	(Come Out, Turtle)
Soy una serpiente	(I Am a Snake)

Rimas y Juegos (Rhymes and Games)

Abuelita de Perú	(Grandma from Perú)
Bate, bate chocolate	(Stir, Stir the Chocolate)
Caracol	(Snail)
Chocolate	(Chocolate)
¿Cuántos años tiene la niña?	(How Old Is the Girl?)
El baile de la gallina	(The Chicken Dance)
El barco se hunde	(The Ship Sinks)
El florón	(The Flower)
El pájaro sin jaula	(The Bird Without a Cage)
El pato	(The Duck)
Gallina colorada	(Red Hen)
Muchos pececitos	(Many Little Fish)
Periquito el bandolero	(The Bandit Parakeet)
Pikachú	(Picachu)
¿Quién se comió el pastel?	(Who Ate the Cake?)
Sana, sana	(Heal, Heal)
Señor Lobo	(Mr. Wolf)
Su, su, su	(Su, Su, Su)
Tierra y mar	(Land and Sea)
Tortillitas	(Little Tortillas)
Va a preparar una ensalada	(They are Going to Make a Salad)

Canciones (Songs)

Buenos días	(Good Morning)
Buenos días, mi maestra	(Good Morning, My Teacher)
Cabeza, cara, hombros, pies	(Head, Face, Shoulders, Feet)
Campanero	(Bell Ringer)
Canto de las vocales	(Vowel Song)
Caracol	(Snail)
Corre, conejito	(Run, Little Rabbit)
Cucú, cucú, cantaba la rana	(Cuckoo, Cuckoo, Sang the Frog)
De colores	(The Colors)
Debajo de un botón	(Under a Button)
Doña Cigüeña	(Doña Cigüena)
El árbol de la montaña	(The Mountain Tree)
El gallo pinto	(The Painted Rooster)
El gatito	(The Kitten)
En el lejano bosque	(In the Faraway Forest)
Estrellita	(Little Star)
Familia Dedo	(Finger Family)
Había un sapo	(There Was a Toad)
Hazlo conmigo	(Do It With Me)
La hormiguita	(The Little Ant)
La lechuza	(The Owl)
La mané	(The Hand)
La pequeña araña	(The Little Spider)
La rana	(The Frog)
La vaca lechera	(The Dairy Cow)
La vaca Lola	(Lola the Cow)
La vaquita	(The Little Cow)
Las calaveras	(The Skeletons)
Las manitos	(The Little Hands)
Las verduras	(The Vegetables)
Los pajaritos	(The Little Birds)
Los patitos	(The Ducklings)
Los pollitos	(The Little Chicks)
Marinero	(Sailor)
Mi burro	(My Donkey)
Panadero	(Baker)
Periquito	(Parakeet)
Pin Pon	(Pin Pon)
Salió la gallina	(The Chicken Came Out)
Salta, mi conejito	(Jump, My Bunny)
Sol, solecito	(Little Sun)
Soy una taza	(I Am a Cup)
Tengo una casita	(I Have a Little House)
Un amigo	(A Friend)
Un elefante (Guatemala)	(An Elephant)
Un elefante (Nicaragua)	(An Elephant)
Vamos a remar	(Let's Row)

Yo me gozo	(I Rejoice)
Jun Ti Sanik*	(The Ant)
Ni Tz'unun*	(The Hummingbird)
Ri Utzil Iwach*	(Greetings)

* Bi'x Pa Ch'ab'el Mayab (Songs in a Mayan language, Kaqchikel)

PREFACE

This book contains 90 songs, singing games, chants, and games that I learned while living in Guatemala and Nicaragua. I lived with families and in communities cumulatively for one year (across five visits) and learned children's music in schools, on playgrounds, and from families. This repertoire belongs to living music traditions. The songs were in current practice and cherished in communities from 2015 to 2020. While the majority of the repertoire is in the Spanish language, a few songs in a Mayan language, Kaqchikel, are included to represent Indigenous voices and traditions. As an outsider to the cultures represented in this book, I share these songs with sensitivity, humility, respect, and only with permissions from the musicians, who were compensated for their work.

This book can be used in families, schools, or community centers and is a comprehensive resource that provides social, cultural, and historic contexts to frame the children's singing traditions. Descriptions of fieldwork sites and singers engaging in musical play are included along with short biographies written by the musicians in Kaqchikel and Spanish and translated into English. Accompanying field videos provide opportunities to witness the songs in authentic contexts, audio recordings help with pronunciation, and additional videos and photographs offer views of towns and regional landscapes. An overview of culturally responsive and sustaining pedagogies is presented with guidance to responsibly embed the songs in classrooms and curriculums. A summary of music in Central America describes how historical events eradicated, shaped, and contributed to the diverse music genres in the area, providing a perspective on how the singing traditions represented in this collection fit into the greater landscape of musical cultures in Central America. To deepen awareness of the stories and legacies of families with heritage in the region, a brief history of Central America presents accounts of first civilizations, colonization, civil war, politics, and current events.

It is with great honor that I have been given permission to share these songs with you. Behind each song is a special memory, and my hope is that you will now create your own. I wish you, your students, and your families joy on this musical journey.

ACKNOWLEDGMENTS

I am deeply grateful to the welcoming communities I lived among in Guatemala and Nicaragua during my song collection journey, which resulted in many meaningful relationships and connections. My first acknowledgment is for the founders and owners of Jabel Tinamit Spanish School, Candelaria and Gregorio, in Guatemala. Their generosity, kindness, support, and professionalism in running a school that offers an exceptional experience in language study and cultural immersion is treasured beyond what my words can express. I offer heartfelt gratitude to María Carmelina Ajcalón, who was extremely gracious in sharing many songs alongside continued advisement and help throughout the writing of this book. She did so with wisdom, grace, and kindness. I thank Gladys García, my first Spanish teacher at the school, with whom I spent countless hours, both in person and online, learning Spanish with a tremendous amount of laughter and joy. I am grateful to other teachers and staff at the school: Antonio, Florinda, Nicolasa, Ingrid, Aracely, Elizabeth, Patricia, Celestina, José, Miquel, and Astrid. The community that they collectively create, nurture, and support will always be held very dear in my family's heart.

The principal and teachers at Escuela Modelo Inclusiva de Educación Infantil in Guatemala graciously welcomed me into their classrooms: Carmen Alicia Hernandéz Mata, Emma Leticia Chávez, Damaris Marely Mogollón Tecun de Santizo, Merlyn Rubí Celada García, Marí, and Luz Adriana Cutillo Mogollón. Because of their generosity, I was able to observe teachers implementing music in their lessons and catch glimpses into education practices in Guatemalan schools. Thank you to La Familia González and La Familia Ical, who shared their homes and music. It was through these homestay experiences that we were able to learn about the lives and cultures of a few Guatemalan families.

I was so fortunate to learn from the teachers at La Mariposa Spanish School in Nicaragua. Asalia Mercado was an outstanding collaborator and contributor, sharing songs and organizing group videos. Lidia Hernández, an exceptional teacher, shared a few chants and also introduced me to her mother, Nora Blass Hernández, whose delightful warmth and presence made her songs so personal and special. I would also like to express gratitude to other teachers and staff at the school: Ricardo, Dariela, Luís, Marcala, Tamar, Marelya, Milder, Maivin, Heydi, Claudia, Clavelioi, Paleska, Brandon, Dariela, Guillermina, Paulette, and Josimar. I have joyful and rich memories of living and studying in this community with my family. Many thanks to the teachers and children at Escuela Pablo Antonio Cuadra, Escuela República de Cuba, and La Mariposa Preschool in Nicaragua, who allowed me the opportunity to observe children's musical play, songs, and playground games. Visits to Escuela La Amistad with Isabel were a highlight as I witnessed her sharing a wealth of songs and singing games with her students over multiple visits.

Acknowledgments

Sucely Puluc, the book illustrator from Guatemala City, has provided beautiful, playful, and thoughtful illustrations that bring joy to the song pages. From the first time we spoke, I was in awe of her vision and commitment to social justice and knew she would be a perfect match for creating artwork to accompany the songs. Nadia Aquilar recorded audio files for the companion website and did so with great attention to detail, professionalism, care, and her beautiful voice.

I owe a debt of gratitude to dear friends and colleagues who were extremely generous with their time, advice, and guidance throughout this project: Dr. Christin Cleaton-Ruiz offered outstanding expertise on the history of Central America, Dr. Terri Griffin provided thoughtful suggestions and guidance regarding culturally responsive and sustaining pedagogies, Carlos and Mary Santiago were thorough and generous with translation help, and Dr. Christopher Roberts provided insightful guidance and recommendations. Thank you also to Colleen Casey-Nelson, Dr. Karen Howard, Dr. Kimberly Muñoz, Liban O. Gómez, Constance Cook, Aimee Curtis Pfitzner, Dr. Felicia Barber, and Jacqueline Sugrue for their help, support, and suggestions. I am also grateful to Westfield State University for supporting my sabbatical and international travel to engage in this work. I feel blessed to work among a community that is incredibly supportive, dedicated, and welcoming.

Thank you to my family for helping with book details. My daughter, Phoebe, contributed the artwork for "Soy una taza," my son, Levi, edited the videos for the companion website, and my husband, Craig, helped with photo editing. I would also like to thank my family for being such wonderful traveling companions. I will always hold dear our time spent together living in Guatemala and Nicaragua.

ABOUT THE COMPANION WEBSITE

www.oup.com/us/cantaconmigo

Oxford University Press has created a website to accompany *¡Canta Conmigo! Songs and Singing Games from Guatemala and Nicaragua*. The website hosts:

Field videos to witness the songs and singing games in authentic contexts and to help with pronunciation. Song histories, variants, and information about field recordings are also discussed.

Studio audio files for additional guidance in pronunciation.

Photographs and field videos of towns, cities, and landscapes for virtual tours and visual contexts. *Field videos* of marimba bands, a folkloric dance performance, a children's choir, and links to active music groups and recording artists are also included.

All links to media files are indicated with the symbol ▶.

PART 1
Suggestions for Teachers and Context

Part 1 includes the following: Suggestions for Teachers provides strategies for how to responsibly teach and include the music into curriculums. Themes discussed include cultural contexts, authentic transmission practices, honoring song histories, Indigenous Music, and culturally responsive and sustaining pedagogies. Living Traditions: Children's Music in Guatemala and Nicaragua reviews children's music traditions and singing cultures in these two countries. Overview: Central America, Guatemala, and Nicaragua includes brief summaries of the region's geography, climate, languages, national instruments, demographics, and economies. Fieldwork Locations describes the sites where songs were learned to set the scenes for repertoire. Biographies, which are written by the informants and presented in English, Spanish, and Kaqchikel, are included to learn about the lives of the musicians who shared music for this book. More thorough discussions about culturally responsive and sustaining teaching, history of Central America, and history of music in Central America can be found in Part 3 of this book.

Suggestions for Teachers

Cultural Connections: Teach the songs in this book to add relevance for students with family heritage in Guatemala and Nicaragua or more generally from nearby Hispanic countries as many songs are shared across regions. Additionally, embed these songs into your classes as a gateway to learning about these musical cultures for those who do not maintain heritage in this region. Avoid assumptions that Hispanic students speak Spanish or are familiar with, identify with, or enjoy traditional music from Hispanic countries. Children from first-, second-, or third-generation families will embrace and express culture in very different ways among and across generations.

Transmission: Teach these songs orally to maintain the authentic mode of transmission and honor child culture by preserving teaching practices maintained for generations before this repertoire entered classrooms. Children learn from each other by through-singing and total immersion as they listen, watch, and join in when ready, and this process should be sustained in the classroom. Children engage in musical play with joyful noise, laughter, negotiations, and acceptance of the breakdown of the games. In a school environment, find a balance between respecting these traditions and classroom expectations to ensure you are teaching music and not obedience. The classroom environment is different from free unstructured time on playgrounds, however, children have been teaching each other singing games without the help of adults for generations, and the transmission process should be not only respected but also considered as best practice.

Language: Sing the songs in the transcribed language, Spanish or Kaqchikel. The English translations are provided to communicate meanings for teachers and students, not as performance practice. Field videos and additional audio files can help with pronunciation.

Cultural Contexts: Presentation of the repertoire should be embedded within visual, geographic, cultural, and historic contexts. Show the landscape pictures and field videos of informants engaging in the songs and singing games to witness the sites and music traditions in authentic contexts. Geographic references using maps can show where each song was performed, making note of the locations of any song variants in this book or shared by children. Discuss how the songs were used in families, schools, and communities, and share any known history to develop an appreciation of their use over time and locations. Written by the singers in Spanish or Kaqchikel and translated into English, biographies of a few contributors and the book illustrator are included to learn about the lives of the individual artists. These can be read aloud to students in any of the languages accessible to the teacher and students.

Song Variants: While using this collection, it is possible that a teacher or student may know a version of a song with melodic, rhythmic, or lyrical variations. This discovery can instigate a conversation about oral folk song traditions and regional dialects. Invite students to teach their variant to the class and discuss the issue that a fixed musical transcription does not adequately represent the flexibility of an oral tradition that embraces variation over time and location. To demonstrate this point, different versions of three songs are included: "Un elefante" and "El patio de mi casa" both have variants from Guatemala and Nicaragua. The two variations of "La pájara pinta" were observed in the same town in Nicaragua.

Journey of the Music: Spanish language songs in this collection have roots in colonialism. The language, melodic and harmonic structures, and select songs were initially brought to the region during the Spanish conquest in the 1500s. Therefore, when teaching the repertoire, pause and contemplate this journey and engage in age-appropriate discussion with students about this history. The chapters "Music in Central America" and "Brief History of Central America" in Part 3 offer summaries of historic themes and describe how past events shaped current music practices.

Indigenous Music: When embedding repertoire in a curriculum to represent a music culture or region, be mindful of including Indigenous music, the first traditions of the land, to avoid further marginalization of these histories and practices. Three songs in this collection are in the Mayan language Kaqchikel, but the melodies are not Indigenous because most have not been preserved. Rather, Indigenous lyrics were set to European or European-derived melodies, thus only maintaining the language. This small number of songs does not represent the great diversity of Indigenous peoples in Central America. There are 28 distinct Maya groups as well as Garifuna and Moskitu cultures in the region, each with distinct languages and customs. These three songs are meant to represent Indigenous voices and to inspire further inquiry, as the main focus of this book is to share children's music in the Spanish language.

Representation: The repertoire in this book represents oral singing traditions in Guatemala and Nicaragua in practice within a greater musical landscape of rich traditions. The chapter on "Music in Central America" is intended as a starting point to explore the diversity of music practices in the region. When teaching a unit on music in Guatemala or Nicaragua, these songs can be integrated into lessons alongside other historic or current genres.

Modifications: It is always best to maintain authentic practices when engaging in the material. However, the repertoire that includes tug-of-wars, tickling, and grabbing might not be suitable for a school classroom and these elements can be omitted or modified as needed.

Discussions: Empower students to participate in age-appropriate discussions that stimulate social, emotional, political, and intellectual growth. Music cultures do not exist in a vacuum and nor should their teaching. Music education must include pedagogical processes that stimulate critical thinking, develop thoughtful citizens, establish a place of belonging, and encourage identity exploration. Engage students in age-appropriate discussions of the history and cultures of Central America. Music always carries a story and it is our obligation to give voice to the journey, history, and people that belong to the traditions.

Culturally Responsive and Sustaining Pedagogies: Teach the repertoire within a framework of culturally responsive and sustaining pedagogies. A summary of these practices, broad suggestions, and materials for further study are provided in the chapter "Culturally Responsive and Sustaining Pedagogies."

Living Traditions
Children's Music in Guatemala and Nicaragua

Children's music traditions have been maintained, shaped, and transmitted orally for generations in families and communities in Nicaragua and Guatemala. An integral part of daily life, singing practices serve many purposes. In families, caregivers sing traditional music, religious songs, ballads, and lullabies as parenting tools to form bonds and affect mood. They also carry out finger plays, bouncing games, hand-clapping rhymes, and made-up songs to engage in musical play with their children. This musical environment fosters the continuity of cultural heritage, beliefs, and history.

Children maintain their own vibrant singing cultures at home, on playgrounds, and in community spaces. During musical play, children immerse themselves in social dynamics as they establish rules, negotiate terms, and learn social norms, all while they develop gross and fine motor skills, engage in artistic expression and improvisation, preserve child culture, and form social bonds. I witnessed several types of songs and games in Guatemala and Nicaragua, including traditional songs, singing games, hand-clapping rhymes, counting-out and elimination games, jump-rope rhymes, chasing games, and responsive movement songs.

Children's music also thrives in schools and daycare settings as teachers use music to create a joyful community, encourage creative expression and responsive movement, communicate expectations, and teach concepts. Recorded music has been integrated into classrooms and digital access allows teachers to play accompaniment to children's singing and activities. Music artists such as CantaJuego from Spain and Dúo Tiempo del Sol from Argentina have albums available on CD and online that were used in the classrooms I visited. For example, the traditional song "Soy una taza" (I Am a Cup) was often performed with recorded music.

Each generation shapes and passes its musical heritage to the next generation, resulting in multiple song variants over time and across locations. Within the same country, area, and even in the same town, different variants may be witnessed. For example, "La pájara pinta" was performed differently by various community members in San Juan de la Concepción, Nicaragua. Some of the songs in this collection are also shared among other Hispanic countries with melodic, rhythmic, and lyric variations such as "Un elefante," "El patio de mi casa," "Los pollitos," "Doña Ana," "Rueda, rueda," and "Que llueva."

Long-standing oral music traditions are evidenced in singing games with historic ties to Spain, such as "Nerón, Nerón," "Doña Ana," "La pájara pinta," and "El patio de mi casa," which also have multiple variants across several Hispanic countries. There are melodies in this collection that can be traced to regions in Europe, such as "El gallo pinto" (France), "En el lejano bosque" (Germany), and five lyrical variants set to the tune of "Frère Jacques" (France): "Buenos días," "Campanero," "La lechuza," and "Panadero" in Spanish and "Ri Utzil Iwach" in Kaqchikel. Whether children are engaging in deep-rooted traditions or newer practices influenced by media sources, children's music and musical play are thriving parts of daily life in Guatemala and Nicaragua.

Children at musical play at Escuela Pablo Antonio Cuadra (Granada, Nicaragua)

Overview

Central America, Guatemala, and Nicaragua

Guatemala and Nicaragua are countries located in Central America along with Belize, El Salvador, Honduras, Costa Rica, and Panama. A thin strip of land in the southernmost region of the continent North America, the isthmus was formed approximately three million years ago by collisions of the earth's tectonic plates, an instability that contributes to the consistent threat of earthquakes and volcanic eruptions. Before colonization began in the 1500s, the region was inhabited by Indigenous groups, most notably the Maya.

Surrounding the region is the Caribbean Sea to the east, the Pacific Ocean to the west, Mexico to the north, and Colombia (South America) to the south. Central America boasts many mountain ranges and fertile valleys where raising livestock and growing crops are common. The lowlands maintain a hot and humid tropical climate, while the highlands are cooler. There are two seasons in Central America, *la temporada seca* (the dry season) and *la temporada lluvia* (the rainy season). While many Indigenous and Creole languages are in current practice, Spanish is the most widely spoken language in all countries except Belize, where English is the official language. The marimba is the national instrument of Guatemala, Nicaragua, and Costa Rica, and a featured instrument in ensemble groups throughout Central America. For a more thorough review of the region, see the chapter "Brief History of Central America."

Guatemala ▶

Guatemala was a Spanish colony for almost three centuries before gaining independence in 1821. The former Mayan settlement *Quauhtemallan* (Land of trees) was pronounced "Guatemala" by the Spanish and used to name the capital city and country. It is the most populous country in Central America with 17.3 million residents, 56 percent of whom are of Indigenous and Spanish descent and 44 percent that identify as Indigenous, which includes Maya, Garifuna, Xinka, and Creole (Afrodescendants). The Maya maintain 28 distinct groups, the largest of which are K'iche, Kaqchikel, Mam, and Q'eqchi'. The majority of the Maya live in the highlands, a series of high valleys between the Sierra Madre de Chiapas mountain range to the south and the Petén lowlands to the north.

Known as *La alma de la tierra* (The soul of the earth), Guatemala is home to 30 volcanos and 14 distinct ecosystems due to the geographical diversity that ranges from mountain chains to coastal plains. The country comprises 22 departments and is further divided into 340 municipalities. Industries include tourism, textiles, clothing, furniture, petroleum, and metals, and the main exports include bananas, coffee, sugar, and vegetables. Discriminatory income distribution practices favor Spanish descendants, which leaves the majority of Indigenous groups living below the poverty line.

Guatemalans have been immigrating north since the 1930s, and approximately 1.4 million Hispanics with Guatemalan ancestry live in the United States. While Guatemalans live in almost every U.S. state, the largest populations are in California, Florida, and Texas, with smaller populations in New York, New Jersey, Maryland, Virginia, North Carolina, Georgia, and Illinois.

Nicaragua ▶

Nicaragua gained its independence from Spain in 1821 and was named after the largest Indigenous settlement, Nicarao, combined with the word *agua* (water), referring to Lago Cocibolca anad Lago Xolotlán, the two largest lakes in the country. It maintains the nickname *La tierra de lagos y volcanes* (The land of lakes and volcanos) with 24 volcanoes and many rivers, lakes, and lagoons. Nicaragua sustains a very high level of biodiversity due to land protection and a variety of habitats that include rainforests, lakes, mountains, and volcanoes. Nicaragua is also known as *La tierra de poetas* (Land of the poets), as the poet and national treasure Rubén Darío (1867–1916) instigated the Spanish-American literary movement known as *modernismo*.

Nicaragua is the largest country in land area in Central America and has a population of 6.2 million residents: 70 percent of Indigenous-Spanish descent, 17 percent White, 9 percent Black, and 5 percent Indigenous (although most Indigenous self-report as Spanish descent due to extreme discrimination). The country comprises 15 departments and two autonomous regions, and it is further divided into 153 municipalities.

The economy relies primarily on agriculture. Nicaragua produces coffee, bananas, sugar cane, rice, and corn and exports coffee, sugar, and meat. Other areas of industry include tourism, textiles, construction, mining, and fisheries. Economically, Nicaragua is the poorest country in Central America with widespread unemployment and poverty. Nicaraguans who choose to emigrate primarily move south to Costa Rica for agricultural work. However, small numbers of Nicaraguans have been immigrating north since the 1900s, predominantly to Florida, California, and Texas, with roughly 350,00 Hispanics of Nicaraguan descent living in the United States.

Fieldwork Locations

This chapter describes fieldwork locations where the songs were learned and provides context for the repertoire in this collection. The songs belong to living music traditions and are cherished by teachers, children, and families in each community. Some identifiers and names have been changed or omitted to protect identities.

Panajachel, Sololá, Guatemala ⏵

Panajachel is a town nestled on Lake Atitlán in the southwestern highlands and offers views of the San Pedro, Tolimán, and Atitlán volcanoes. The region is predominantly Mayan and home to the Kaqchikel and Tz'utujil Indigenous groups who have maintained their languages, customs, and connection to ancestral land for thousands of years. Panajachel, which roughly translates to "place of the matasanos" (white sapote fruit trees), is situated among nature reserves and rural hill towns. A large outdoor market boasts a colorful display of fruits and vegetables for sale; potatoes, peppers, cucumbers, carrots, avocados, and lychees recently harvested from local farms fill the stalls. One vendor selling freshly picked coconuts will, upon request, slice the top off with a large knife and insert a straw for a refreshing drink. The busy street Calle Santander is lined with restaurants, small hotels, and shops where artisans sell colorful tapestries, quilts, oil paintings, bags, clothing, and souvenirs. The street ends at the lake where *lanchas* (water taxis) are available to shuttle passengers to nearby lakeside towns, including Santa Cruz, Jaibalito, San Marcos, San Pedro, Santiago, and Santa Catarina. Well known for its beauty and rich history, the town is a destination for world travelers as well as Guatemalans seeking respite from the busy capital city.

Jabel Tinamit Spanish School ▶

The school is located on Callejón las Armonias (Harmony Alley), surrounded by houses and small stores. Antonio's warm greeting, ¡adelante! (come in!), at the school's entrance sets a tone for the welcoming environment. While enjoying morning coffee and cookies from *la panadaría* (the bakery), teachers and students socialize in the school lounge underneath the cascading *tumbergias* (Bengal clockvine), long hanging plants that attract and nourish *los colibrís* (hummingbirds). Jabel Tinamit (beautiful town) is a Maya-owned and family-managed business. Candelaria and Gregorio, a married couple, started the business in 1998 and have created a nurturing community for students from many parts of the world to visit and engage in Spanish or Kaqchikel language study. The school also provides opportunities to learn about Maya culture during afternoon school activities. The teachers give cooking classes on how to prepare traditional Guatemalan dishes such as *pepián*, *pulique*, and *paches*. They also offer weaving demonstrations, show historical documentaries, lead hikes on local trails, and organize tours to visit markets, artisans, museums, and churches.

On the sun-filled *terrazzo* (rooftop) of the school with beautiful views of the town, Carmelina, Nicolasa, and Florinda shared many songs and singing games, including "Campanita de oro" (Golden Bell), "Señor Lobo" (Mr. Wolf), "Los pollitos" (The Little Chicks), and "Periquito" (Parakeet). They sang, laughed, and reminisced while engaging in the musical play from their childhood. Their chatting during song demonstrations was a seamless dance between Kaqchikel and Spanish, their first and second languages.

In a school classroom overlooking the garden, Carmelina shared several more songs that she sings with young children in Spanish classes. With a tender voice, she sang "Un amigo" (A Friend) and "Juguemos en el bosque" (Let's Play in the Forest). In the school garden, Ingrid demonstrated "El pato" (The Duck), a chant with *una dinámica* (actions), and commented that she engages in this playful activity with her son. Her performance of this delightful chant is a treasured part of this collection.

It is important to consider that the Mayan instructors are teaching the language and songs of their oppressors. While most visitors to this school learn Spanish for personal enrichment, the Maya were forced to learn the language under Spanish colonial rule or, after independence, for educational and economic advancement.

Escuela Modelo Inclusiva de Educación Infantil (Inclusive Model School of Early Childhood Education) ▶

Located at the end of Callejón El Capulín (Cherry Alley), the open-air school features a welcoming courtyard for children's play with colorfully painted walls and lush plants. A surrounding circle of eight classrooms accommodates children four to eight years old, dynamic teachers, and a few student teachers. The children attend school either in the morning or the afternoon and wear a school uniform of maroon pants or skirt and a white top. Damaris and her class playfully engaged in "Las calaveras" (The Skeletons) and moved responsively to the lyrics. Adriana led her class in "Soy una serpiente" (I Am a Snake) as she and the children weaved around the schoolyard to a variety of tempos. Rubí traveled to each classroom to sing, dance, and engage in movement activities with the students, and played "Muchos pecesitos" (Many Little Fish) as the sharks chased and tagged the little fish. Laughter abounded in the school with the joyful inclusion of music throughout the school day. While there is no formal music education in public schools in Guatemala, most teachers integrate singing into classes with a variety of teaching objectives, such as responsive and gross motor movement, community building, and play. (See the chapter "Biographies" for background on teachers Damaris Mogollón and Merlyn Rubí Celada García.)

La Familia González

Down a narrow alley off Callejón La Navidad (Christmas Alley), where children gather to play *fútbol* (soccer) and other games, my family (me, my husband, and two children ages 8 and 10) lived with the González family in a large three-story cement block house. With three children of their own, ages 1, 6, and 12, we shared meals together with laughter, storytelling, and occasional singing. Paula, the mother, cooked traditional meals that included rice, beans, tamales, fried plantains with cream, and vegetables from the local market. Minutes before sitting down together, a tall hot stack of freshly made tortillas was purchased from the corner *tortillería* to accompany the meal. The family collectively recalled the melody and actions to the singing game "Ronda el campanario." They also energetically sang "Vamos a remar" and "Campanero" set to the melodies of "Row, Row, Row Your Boat" and "Frère Jacques."

La Familia Ical

We lived with *la familia* Ical (the Ical family) in a yellow stucco house on the busy Calle Principal (Main Street). While raising three children ages 7, 13, and 15, the father worked in construction and the mother ran a used clothing store in their front yard. During mealtimes, the family shared the songs and singing games "El toro toronjil," "Ronda de la mano," and "El gallo pinto." Presentations came in the form of melodic fragments and corrections from multiple family members, all with joyous interruptions and laughter.

Buena Vista, Guatemala

Standing on María Carmelina Ajcalón's family land in Buena Vista (which means Good View), towering volcanoes and Lake Atitlán can be seen in the distance. Carmelina's ancestors were the first inhabitants of this Mayan town in the early 1900s. The town now has a population of around 600. Primary occupations are construction and agriculture and nearby fields produce onions, corn, beans, potatoes, broccoli, tomatoes, chili pimentos, and herbs. Carmelina wore a *güipil* (Mayan blouse), a handwoven garment with patterns that represented her town. Singing in Kaqchikel, Carmelina shared a few songs in her first language that she learned in elementary school. "Jun Ti Sanik" (The Ant),

"Ni Tz'unun" (The Hummingbird), and "Ri Utzil Iwach" (Greetings) are set to European-derived or -inspired melodies. Most of the Indigenous music was lost after the Spanish conquest. (See the chapter "Biographies" for more about María Carmelina Ajcalón.)

Granada, Nicaragua ▶

Granada was first home to the Indigenous settlement of Xalteva, where the Chorotega culture resided. The Spanish arrived in the 1500s and seized land to construct colonial cities. The majority of the Indigenous population did not survive. Granada was built in 1524 with Parque Colón de Granada (Granada's Columbus Park), named after Cristobal Colón (Christopher Columbus), at the heart of the city center. The park is shaded by palm, ficus, mango, and poinciana trees, and features a large fountain, an outdoor restaurant, brightly painted horse-drawn carriages around the periphery, and vendors selling ice cream, souvenirs, and jewelry. Painted a vibrant yellow, Catedral de Nuestra Señora de la Asunción (Our Lady of the Assumption Cathedral) towers over one side of the park. Casa de los Tres Mundos (House of the Three Worlds), a cultural arts center that houses schools for music, art, and dance, is located nearby. The popular thoroughfare Calle La Calzada (Calzada Street) starts at the park and ends at Lago Colcibolca (Colcibolca Lake). It is lined with colorfully painted storefronts, restaurants, ice cream shops, and small hotels. A large outdoor city market features an intricate maze of narrow corridors where vendors sell vegetables, fruit, legumes, rice, beans, spices, clothing, shoes, and household items. Some vendors peddle their wares on carts throughout the city, each with their own street cry melodically advertising their products for sale. Fresh papayas, avocados, plantains, bananas, broccoli, and carrots are some of the items that are widely available.

Escuela Pablo Antonio Cuadra ▶

This open-air elementary school for grades 1 through 6 is located in the northern section of Granada. It was named after Pablo Antonio Cuadra (1912–2002), a famous Nicaraguan poet, playwright, and graphic artist. Nicaraguan children attend school either in the morning or afternoon and wear a school uniform of blue skirt or pants and a white top, which represent the sea and sky. Teachers might start and end the day with songs, however there is no formal system of music education in the public schools. A paved yard at the school entry is a designated space for school assemblies and recess, where children spontaneously engage in musical play. Jump-rope chants, hand-clapping rhymes, singing games, and chasing games are a daily part of recess. While observing "¿Cuántos años tiene la niña?" and "El barco se hunde," children demonstrated that they were in charge of their own play as they negotiated rules, mandated expectations, and held each other accountable. The transmission and continuity of their childhood culture was in full bloom.

La Familia Paéz

The Paéz family lives in a large house on Parque Xalteva (Xalteva Park) where the mother, Johana, teaches English to those interested in achieving basic to advanced language skills to expand employment opportunities in sectors such as tourism and call centers. Johana and her daughter provided cheerful demonstrations of a few childhood singing game such as "Rueda, rueda," "Que llueva," and "Doña Ana." They joyously played together and described games in the large open-air courtyard of their house.

Sarahí

Sarahí, a teacher at Mía Spanish School, a small family owned and operated language center in downtown Granada, shared two songs that she enjoyed singing with her 2-year-old daughter. "Estrellita" is a Spanish-language variant of "Twinkle, Twinkle Little Star" and "Panadero" is set to "Frère Jacques."

San Juan de la Concepción, Nicaragua

At an elevation of approximately 700 meters (2,300 feet) above sea level, San Juan de la Concepción maintains a cooler and less humid climate than the lowland city of Granada. This agricultural region produces oranges, lemons, pineapples, *plátanos* (plantains), and *pitahaya* (dragon fruit). The small downtown has a variety of *tiendas* (stores), a large playing field where children and teenagers play *fútbol* (soccer), (not sure "the" is needed in front of the Spanish name?) Escuela República de Cuba, and La Mariposa Spanish Language School and Eco-Hotel.

La Mariposa Spanish School and Eco-Hotel ▶

This exceptional school was founded with a strong commitment to Spanish language education, cultural immersion, sustaining local employment, providing community services, social justice, animal rescue, and preserving the environment. The school attracts international travelers and is situated on a beautiful nature reserve among coffee plants, banana trees, birdlife, and butterflies. The cooks prepare savory meals made with fresh vegetables from their organic gardens or local farms, and dedicated teachers engage with students in one-on-one Spanish lessons in outdoor classrooms throughout the nature reserve.

Asalia, a dynamic and energetic teacher, sang "Yo me gozo" (I Rejoice) and thoughtfully described and demonstrated the children's hand-clapping game "Tortillitas" (Little Tortillas). With a group of teachers at the school, she engaged in several traditional singing games, including "Nerón, Nerón," "Rueda, rueda," and "Doña Ana." It was evident that these singing games fostered community through their playful and heartfelt performances. Lidia chanted "Gallina colorada" (Red Hen) and "Sana, sana" (Heal, Heal), a phrase that parents share with children who are hurt or sick. She also generously took me to her house down the street to meet her mother, Nora Blas Hernández, who shared her treasured song collection. (See "Biographies" for more information about Asalia Janeth Mercado Moraga.)

Nora Blass Hernández ▶

Nora, a retired elementary school teacher, acquired a large repertoire of songs during teacher-training workshops, which she integrated into her classes. We sat on her sun-filled patio surrounded by shrubs, flowers, and singing birds as she flipped through her notebook of handwritten lyrics and sang. Nora thoughtfully described and demonstrated *las dinámicas* (the actions) that accompanied each song. While singing "Las manitos" (The Little Hands), she improvised lyrics and movements to demonstrate different activities we can do with our hands such as eating, writing, and bathing. She sang "Canto de las vocales," which teaches vowel sounds. She also shared "De colores" (The Colors), "La hormiguita" (The Ant), "Salió la gallina," and several other songs. Her gentle and welcoming demeanor added warmth to each song, many of which are featured throughout this book. (See "Biographies" for more information about Nora Blas Hernández.)

La Mariposa Preschool

Supported by La Mariposa Spanish School, this small neighborhood preschool is located in the teacher's home. Dariela, a dynamic and energetic instructor, engaged in musical play with the children to foster community and promote joy. She and her students sang and moved to "Soy una taza" (I Am a Cup), an infectious song that was sweeping the country. The children performed a rapid and joyous sequence of movements with a recording by the group CantaJuego from Spain. It was evident that media played a role in the musical lives of children and in schools.

Escuela República de Cuba ▶

This small elementary school is painted white and blue to represent the sea and sky. The school entrance boasts *Sacuanjoche* trees with the national flower in full bloom; the name is derived from the Náhuatl language meaning "flower with beautiful yellow petals." Inside a first-grade classroom, a teacher sang "Los pajaritos" (The Little Birds) with the children as they playfully created actions to represent different animals. The students also shared and dramatized the poem "Caracol" (Snail). Reciting poetry is common in schools and families and is a source of national pride inspired by the famous Nicaraguan poet Rubén Darío. (1867–1916)

Masaya, Nicaragua ▶

Known as *la cuna de folklore nicaragüense* (the cradle of Nicaraguan folklore), Masaya is a city known for its gifted artisans and folkloric culture. The National Artisan Market, a bustling outdoor venue, features aisles of vendors selling locally made pottery, hammocks, paintings, and woodcarvings. A centrally located stage features local troupes that present historic folk dances such as "El Güegüense" (Wise Man), a signature postcolonial folkloric dance that mocks the Spanish and protests colonial rule. The city is also a gateway to the Masaya Volcano National Park, the largest national park in the country, where visitors can walk up to the crater of the active volcano to observe continuous emissions of sulfur dioxide and the incandescent glow of the lava lake.

Escuela La Amistad (The Friendship School) ▶

Escuela La Amistad is a two-room schoolhouse nestled in a small neighborhood in Masaya. Constructed with bricks and a red metal roof, children ages four to six enjoyed the dedicated instruction of Isabel, who integrated many songs and singing games into her teaching.

The young children lined up as little ducklings behind Isabel, the mother duck, weaving around the room and singing "Los patitos" (The Ducks). They engaged in the playful game "¿Quién se comió el pastel?" (Who Ate the Cake?) as they called on each other to take turns in the chant. They also engaged lyrical improvisation while playing the traditional singing game "Doña Ana" and sang several other songs, such as "En el lejano bosque" (In the Faraway Forest), "Mi burro" (My Donkey), and "Sol solecito" (Little Sun). Isabel sang the additive song "El árbol de la montaña" (The Mountain Tree) in the backyard of the school as the children played. Isabel is deeply connected to the folkloric music culture of Nicaragua and shares that passion with her students.

Biographies

Each cherished song in this collection was shared with me by teachers, children, or a family that I got to know while living in Guatemala and Nicaragua. Several musicians and the illustrator wrote short biographies to introduce themselves, which were written in Spanish and have been translated into English. María Carmelina Ajcalón also wrote hers in her first language, Kaqchikel.

María Carmelina Ajcalón, Buena Vista, Guatemala

Nub'i rin María Carmelina. 31 nujuna, xi nalax pa jun ko'ol tinamit rub'I jab'el nu wachin (Buena Vista) xinalax pa jun ch'alal' ri'il mayab, chiri k'owa jab'el taq na'oj choqa pixä. Nuch'alal ri'il kowan ko'ol, ye k'o ka'i nu chaq', roj oxi ixoqi, majunta nuxib'al. Roj yoj ch'o ka'i ch'abal kaxlan ch'abal choqa mayab ch'abal Kaqchiquel.

    Taq rin ko'ol kowan xin wil ri k'ewal taq xib'e pa tijob'al ruma ri ixoqi ojer manyeb'a ta pa tijob'al, rin, yikuj ixoq rumari xinkis ri nutijob'al, runaj xinkis ruma ri k'ayewal, wakame rin jun ixoq k'o nutamab'al.Tajin yi samaj pa jun tijob'al ruchin kaxlan ch'abal k'o q'ij nink'ut ri mayab ch'ab'al (Kaqchiquel).

    Rin xi k'ule' taq k'o 29 nujuna' wakame k'o jun nunëy kaji rati't. Ri yich'o oxi ch'ab'al Kaqchikel, Español choqa inglés nuwajo nuk'ut rich'abal chuwach wal. Rin ninb'ij yach'o pa ninkaj chik ch'ab'al chanin nawil a samaj, nusamaj wakame riyi'on q'ij chuwa nintamaj kiwach nink'aj winaq chik.

Taj majnuta nusamaj nuqa chinwach yi b'ixaq pa Español choqa pa Kaqchikel, nuqa chinwach ninb'an t'isön. Nutat kowan ye kikot wik'e kama ruma rin kowan yisamaj choga tajin ninkut ütz na'oj chikiwal ri q'opoji choqa ixoqi. Wakama yek'ij q'opoji yeb'enaq pa tijob'al rumari kowan yinkikot kima riye, ri k'e ri tij'ob'al riye nkiwil jun ütz k'aslen.

Me llamo María Carmelina y tengo 31 años. Vivo en un area rural y nací en un pequeño pueblo se llama Buena Vista y tiene una vista maravillosa. Crecí en una familia Maya donde hay buenos modales y buena educación. Mi familia es muy pequeña. Solo somos tres hermanas, no tengo hermano. Mi familia habla dos idiomas: español y kaqchikel.

Cuando era pequeña, era un poco dificil estudiar, porque no era común para las mujeres estudiar, pero yo fui muy valiente, y pude terminar mi educación. Terminé un poco tarde, pero fue posible. Ahora soy una mujer profesional. Trabajo en *Jabel Tinamit Spanish Schoo*l (una escuela de español) y algunas veces enseño kaqchikel.

Me casé a los 29 años y ahora tengo un bebé de 10 meses. Yo hablo tres idiomas: kaqchikel, español, e inglés y me gustaría enseñar esos idiomas a mi hijo. Para mí, hablar muchos idiomas puedes tener muchas oportunidades de trabajo. Con el trabajo que tengo, he conocido a muchas personas de diferentes paises.

En mi tiempo libre me gusta cantar canciones infantiles cortas en español y kaqchikel, también me gusta hacer manualidades y artesanías con materiales de Guatemala. Mis padres están muy felices y orgullosos por mi porque yo soy muy trabajadora y empoderada. También estoy dando buenos ejemplos a otras niñas y mujeres. En la actualidad hay muchas niñas que estudian y eso me hace felíz porque con la educación ellas pueden tener una vida mejor.

My name is María Carmelina. I am 31 years old and I live in the country. I was born in a small town called Buena Vista, which has a wonderful view. I grew up in a Mayan family; we are polite and well-mannered. My family is very small. We are three sisters; I have no brothers. My family speaks two languages: Spanish and Kaqchikel.

When I was little, it was a little difficult to go to school, because not very many women studied, but I was very persistent and was able to finish my education. I finished a little late, but it was possible. I am a career woman now. I work at Jabel Tinamit Spanish School (a Spanish language school) and sometimes I teach Kaqchikel.

I married at 29 and have a 10-month-old baby. I speak three languages—Kaqchikel, Spanish, and English—and I would like to teach those languages to my son. In my experience, speaking several languages provides you with many professional opportunities. In my present position, I have met many people from different countries.

I like to sing short children's songs in Spanish and Kaqchikel in my free time. I also enjoy creating arts and crafts with local materials from Guatemala. My parents are pleased with and proud of me, because I am very hardworking and empowered. I am a good role model for women and girls in my community. Today many girls go to school, and that makes me happy, because with an education they have a better life.

Carmelina contributed the following songs: El gatito, El patio de mi casa, Juguemos en el bosque, La pequeña araña, La vaca lechera, Que llueva, Señor lobo, Un amigo, Un elefante, Jun Ti Sanik, Ni Tzunun, Periquito, Ri Utzil Iwach

Merlyn Rubí Celada García, Panajachel, Guatemala

Soy Merlyn Rubí Celada García, tengo 22 años de edad y soy guatemalteca. Mi profesión me acredita como maestra de educación infantil y me estuve especializando durante tres años en problemas de aprendizaje. Actualmente continúo especializándome en una Licenciatura en Psicopedagogía, por lo cual es evidente que me apasiona el área educativa ya que me motiva en gran manera poder ser parte del cambio positivo y necesario para nuestra educación.

En este escrito, quiero plasmar la importancia de la música en la educación. Inicié este hermoso trayecto laborando en un centro de asistencia para personas con discapacidad, lugar, en el cual fui descubriendo la importancia de la música para el desarrollo de diversas habilidades que nos permiten expresar propiamente la dicha de ser seres humanos. Continué experimentando y comprobando los múltiples beneficios de la música conforme iba adentrándome más a la educación. Tuve la oportunidad de laborar en un centro educativo en el área del nivel preprimario, en el cual cumplía la ardua función de ser profesora de educación musical, descubriendo por cuenta propia la gran influencia de la música en la cotidianidad de los más pequeños. Me permitía integrar diversas áreas a la vez de forma divertida e interactiva, logrando un aprendizaje significativo para quienes consideramos los más pequeños en edad pero realmente gigantes en imaginación, pues todo ello desata diversas emociones innatas que nos indican que la música es fundamental para nuestro desarrollo.

Quiero dejar una brecha amplia para invitarles a seguir haciendo uso de la música sin miedos a la equivocación ya que forma parte del camino el ir descubriendo lo bueno que aporta a cada uno de sus estudiantes, siempre tomando en cuenta la razón de nuestra hermosa profesión que nos permite ir dejando huellas en la vida de tantas personas de una manera muy significativa.

¡¡Que viva la música, que viva para darnos más vida!!

I am Merlyn Rubí Celada García. I am 22 years old and Guatemalan. I am a certified teacher of early childhood education with a specialization in learning disabilities. At present, I am pursuing a degree in educational psychology because I am passionate about the field and inspired to be part of the positive and necessary change for our education.

I want to stress the importance of music in education. I started this beautiful journey working in an assistance center for people with disabilities, a place where I discovered the importance of music for developing skills and allowing us to express what it means to be human. I continued to explore the multiple benefits of music as I continued my career. I had the opportunity to work in a preschool educational center as a music teacher and discovered the importance and influence of music in the daily lives of young children. It allowed me to integrate different knowledge areas in a fun and interactive way and achieve significant learning for those who are small but true giants in imagination. All of this indicates that music is fundamental to our development because it unleashes various innate emotions.

I want to open a space where you can continue making music without the fear of making mistakes, since that is part of the journey of the discovery of its value for students, always considering that the reason for our beautiful profession is that it allows us to impact the lives of so many people in significant ways.

Long live music—may it live and give us more life!

Rubí contributed the following songs: El patio de mi casa, La rana, Muchos pececitos

Damaris Mogollón, Panajachel, Guaremala

Nací en el Departamento de Sololá, el 15 de enero del año 1982. Con 38 años de edad, soy hija de Joaquín Ernesto Mogollón Amézquita y de Thelma Nohemí Mogollón Tecun. Estudié mi nivel académico diversificado en el Colegio Integral Sololateco en el año 2000 y el Técnico en Trabajo Social, en el año 2004, en la Universidad Mariano Gálvez de Guatemala. Contraje matrimonio con Jorge Baudilio Santizo Motta el 5 de febrero del año 2005, soy madre de dos hijos, Jorge Eduardo Santizo Mogollon de 14 años de edad y de José Daniel Santizo Mogollón de 12 años. En el año 2002 empiezo mi carrera de docente en la Escuela Cooperativa el Tablón Sololá, posteriormente, en el Municipio de San José Chacaya, en la Escuela Paín, año 2004, en el año 2005 en la Escuela Oficial Urbana Mixta Tipo Federación, José Vitelio Ralón C, en su Jornada Verpertina, en el año 2006 en la Escuela Oficial de Párvulos Demetria Linares, del 2006 hasta la fecha, en la Escuela Oficial de Párvulos en su Jornada Verpertina, Panajachel, Sololá.

I was born in the Department of Sololá on January 15, 1982. I am 38 years old and the daughter of Joaquín Ernesto Mogollón Amézquita and Thelma Nohemí Mogollón Tecun. I graduated from the Colegio Integral Sololateco in 2000 and earned an associates degree in social work at the Universidad Mariano Gálvez de Guatemala in 2004. I married Jorge Baudilio Santizo Motta on February 5, 2005. I am the mother of two children: Jorge Eduardo Santizo Mogollon, who is 14 years old, and José Daniel Santizo Mogollón, who is 12 years old. In 2002, I started my teaching career. I have taught at the following schools: Escuela Cooperativa el Tablón Sololá, Municipio de San José Chacaya, Escuela Paín, Escuela Oficial Urbana Mixta Tipo Federación, José Vitelio Ralón C, Escuela Oficial de Párvulos Demetria Linares, and at the Escuela Oficial de Párvulos during the afternoon turn in Panajachel, Sololá.

Damaris contributed the following songs: Corre conejito, Doña Ciguena, El pato, Las calaveras, Pin Pon, Un elefante

Nora Blass Hernández, San Juan de la Concepción, Nicaragua

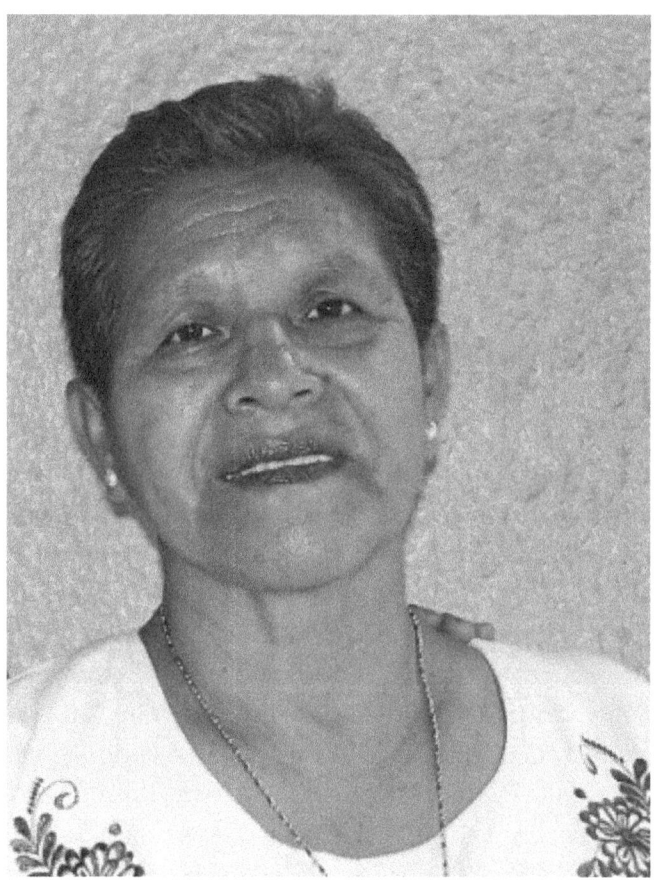

¡Hola a todos! Soy Nora Blass, originaria de San Juan de La Concepción, Masaya, Nicaragua. Cursé mis estudios de profesionalización en la Escuela Normal Ricardo Morales Avilés de la ciudad de Jinotepe, Carazo. Mi experiencia como profesora de educación primaria fue muy bonita.

Desde pequeña me gustaban los cantos religiosos especialmente los de navidad, luego formé parte del coro de la iglesia del pueblo. En mi experiencia como voluntaria en la gran cruzada nacional de alfabetización de adulto, adquirí habilidades que me ayudaron en mi profesión como docente.

Trabajé para el Ministerio de Educción Pública por veintiocho años impartiendo clases a niños de seis a diez años, en los niveles de primero a cuarto y multigrado; impartiendo todas las materias. Usaba muchas dinámicas que incluían cantos que me permitían mantener a los niños activos en la clase de forma disciplinada y ordenada. También me ayudaban a promover la participación inclusiva de todos, más aún de los niños que eran tímidos.

Los cantos que utilizaba en mi trabajo como docente fueron recopilados a través de los años y de acuerdo al grado que impartía, estos me sirvieron como buena herramienta para introducir o desarrollar el tema de cada clase. Además, las materias estaban diseñadas a través de una metodología lúdica que incluía elementos visuales, corporales en general como gestuales en particular; en la que los niños aprendían con mayor facilidad, desarrollaban habilidades y destrezas. Utilizaba por ejemplo los títeres, láminas ilustrativas, juegos y materiales del medio (semillas y hojas de la comunidad). Todo esto despertaba en los estudiantes el interés por aprender.

Fomentaba en mis estudiantes la importancia de conservar nuestra cultura, especialmente cantos y bailes del folclore típico nicaragüense, razón por la cual participaban en los actos matutinos cada semana en la escuela. También, de forma ocasional preparaba a los estudiantes con dramatizaciones de los personajes representativos de nuestra identidad nacional.

Después de jubilarme, los niños de la comunidad me recuerdan como la profesora paciente y alegre, demostrando su estima, aprecio y respeto hacia mí. Siento gran satisfacción al verlos convertidos en personas de bien, el saber que mi dedicación y esfuerzo que hacía en cada clase valió mucho; pues, yo aprendí de ellos también, porque como dice el dicho enseñar es aprender.

Hello everyone! I am Nora Blass and I live in San Juan de La Concepción, Masaya, Nicaragua. I completed my professional studies at Escuela Normal Ricardo Morales Avilés (the Ricardo Morales Teacher's College) in the city of Jinotepe, Carazo. My experience as a primary school teacher was very beautiful.

As a small girl, I liked religious songs, especially Christmas songs, and I was part of the town church choir. In my experience as a volunteer in La Gran Cruzada Nacional de Alfabetización de Adulto (Great National Adult Literacy Crusade) I learned skills that helped me as a teacher.

I worked for the Ministry of Public Education for 28 years teaching children from 6 to 10 years of age; I taught all subjects from first grade through fourth grade, and multi-age classes. I implemented many activities that included singing, which allowed me to keep children active in class in a disciplined and orderly manner. Songs also helped me to promote inclusive participation by everyone, especially children who were shy.

The songs that I used in my teaching were collected over the years, organized according to the grade I taught, and served as tools to introduce or develop lessons for each class. In addition, the classes were designed through game-based pedagogy, which included visual elements and fine and gross motor movements that helped children develop skills and abilities and to learn more easily. For example, I used puppets, illustrations, games, and materials from the environment (seeds and leaves from nature). All this excited the children about learning.

I instilled the importance of preserving our culture in my students, especially Nicaraguan folk songs and dances, which were performed at morning school assemblies each week. I also occasionally directed school plays that were based on important national figures.

Now that I am retired, the children of the community remember me as a patient and cheerful teacher and show their esteem, appreciation, and respect for me. I take great satisfaction in seeing them become responsible, kind, and just citizens, knowing that my dedication and effort in each class was worth a great deal. Well, I learned from them, too, because as the saying goes, teaching is learning.

Nora contributed the following songs: Buenos días mi maestra, Canto de las vocales, De colores, La lechuza, La hormiguita, Las manitos, La vaquita, Las verduras, Salió la gallina

Asalia Janeth Mercado Moraga, San Juan de la Concepción, Nicaragua

De origen nicaragüense, nací el 18 septiembre, 1990, en un municipio llamado La Concepción, departamento de Masaya. Estudié la primaria y secundaria en el *Colegio Bautista*, de la misma localidad. Soy hija de padres muy trabajadores, mi madre Debora Moraga Acosta, de profesión Diseñadora de ropa y mi Padre German Andres Mercado Castaño, de profesión Mecánico. Soy licenciada en *Marketing*.

Soy la hija mayor de cinco hermanos. Desde niña ayudaba a mi mamá a trabajar en la máquina de coser y soñaba con crecer y ayudar a las personas de pocos ingresos económicos, por eso estudié la carrera de *Marketing* y me especialicé en *Enseñanza del Idioma Inglés* en *La Universidad Centroamericana* (UCA-Managua). A los 22 años tuve la oportunidad de graduarme como profesora de español en la *Escuela La Mariposa*, ubicada en San Juan de La Concepción, Masaya, Nicaragua. Impartí clases de español a extranjeros, luego empecé a trabajar en un *call center*, ya que me generaba mayores ingresos económicos.

Siendo mi pasión la enseñanza y el canto, decidí hacer trabajos voluntarios para enseñar a niños el idioma inglés y también en temporadas visitaba la escuela de español *La Mariposa* para dirigir grupos de clases para niños.

Me caracterizo por ser una joven dinámica, creativa, alegre, de corazón noble y con ánimos de superación, para mí, el "No puedo," no existe, haciéndome una persona super positiva ante cualquier situación.

Entre mis sueños están casarme y formar una familia, viajar y enseñar la cultura de Nicaragua en muchos lugares, hacer sentir a mis estudiantes y personas a mi alrededor la magia de la felicidad al cantar y aprender de forma divertida.

I was born in Nicaragua on September 18, 1990, in a municipality called La Concepción in the district of Masaya, where I attended elementary school and high school at Colegio Bautista. I am the daughter of very hard-working parents: my mother, Debora Moraga Acosta, is a clothing designer by profession and my father, German Andres Mercado Castaño, is a mechanic. I hold a bachelor's degree in marketing.

I am the oldest sister of five siblings. As a child, I helped my mother working on the sewing machine and dreamed of growing up and helping people with low incomes, so I studied marketing and specialized in English language teaching at Universidad Centroamericana, UCA-Managua. At 22, I had the opportunity to work as a Spanish teacher at La Mariposa School, located in San Juan de La Concepción, Masaya, Nicaragua. I taught Spanish to foreigners, then I began working in a call center as it generated greater income and allowed me to continue teaching part time.

With my passion for teaching and singing, I decided to be part of a volunteer team to teach children English and to visit La Mariposa School to lead classes for groups of children. I am a dynamic, creative, and cheerful person who likes to challenge myself and overcome obstacles. For me, the words, "I can't," do not exist; I am a super-positive person.

Among my dreams are getting married and starting a family, traveling, teaching Nicaraguan culture in many settings, and making students and people around me feel the magic and happiness of singing and learning in a dynamic way.

Asalia contributed the following songs: Abuelita de Perú, Doña Ana, El florón, El patio de mi casa, Familia Dedo, La pájara pinta, Nerón, Nerón, Que llueva, Rueda, rueda, Soy una serpiente, Soy una taza, Tortillitas, Un elefante, Yo me gozo

Patricia Sucely Puluc Tecúm (illustrator)

Mujer maya k'iche', ilustradora de 24 años, originaria de Chuwila'/Chichicastenango, Quiché, estudiante de Trabajo Social, en la Universidad de San Carlos de Guatemala.

La ilustración me permite encontrar una manera de decodificar la memoria y la territorialidad de mi cuerpo político. Me ilustro, como proceso necesario de encuentro y reconocimiento de mi palabra y la colectividad en la ciencia y tecnología de los pueblos originarios. Mis ilustraciones también se basan en la reivindicación de mi identidad política e histórica; en la denuncia del racismo, el machismo. En mi camino reconozco las memorias de otras mujeres mayas: mis abuelas k'ich'e's, kaqchikeles y mis amigas, hermanas.

En el 2015 realicé mi primera intervención en pared junto al *Colectivo El Papel* reivindicando la memoria de mujeres masacradas durante el genocidio en Guatemala. Soy parte de la colectiva *Niñas Furia –NF*, que aglutina a mujeres de diversos territorios, que, a través de sus procesos y capacidad de creación en la pintura, están tomando espacios desde nosotras y para nosotras. Colaboro con varios colectivos y movimientos mayas, porque creo firmemente que la lucha contra el capitalismo, el patriarcado y el racismo/colonialismo debe ser una lucha interseccional. Mis ilustraciones han sido impresas para campañas preventivas de violencia contra la mujer, material educativo sobre sexualidad y en manuales sobre agroecología.

Maya K'iche woman, 24-year-old illustrator, originally from Chuwila'/ Chichicastenango, Quiché, social work student at the University of San Carlos de Guatemala.

Illustration provides me a way to decipher the historic memory and the territoriality of my political self. I illustrate my selfhood, as a necessary process of discovering and acknowledging my language (word) and communal Indigenous science and technology. My art vindicates my political and historical identity through denouncing racism and patriarchy. In my journey, I honor the memories of other Mayan women: my k'ich'e grandmothers, kaqchikeles, and friends and sisters.

In 2015, I completed my first mural with the Colectivo El Papel in the memory of women massacred during the genocide in Guatemala. I belong to La Colectiva Niñas Furia, which brings women together from different territories to take spaces for ourselves through our calling for and the process of mural painting and other arts. I collaborate with various collectives and Mayan movements because I firmly believe that the fight against capitalism, patriarchy, racism, and colonialism must be an intersectional fight. My illustrations have been printed for preventive campaigns against violence against women, educational material on sexuality, and in manuals on agroecology.

PART 2
La Música (The Music)

This part contains 90 joyful songs learned on playgrounds, in classrooms, and from families and teachers. The repertoire allows for musical play and movement, encourages lyrical improvisation, and fosters community. The collection is organized into three categories: *Rondas* (Singing games), *Rimas y Juegos* (Chants and games), and *Canciones* (Songs). *Canciones*, which comprises 51 songs, includes many pieces with accompanying actions as well as three religious songs and three in a Mayan language, Kaqchikel. *La Musica* includes song transcriptions, game or movement directions, English translations, informant and location citations, brief notes on song histories or performance practice, and illustrations by the Mayan artist Sucely Puluc. Field video, audio recordings, and additional song information on the companion website allow teachers and students to witness the songs in authentic contexts, demonstrate singing games, guide in pronunciation, and learn more about the history of the songs.

Rondas
(Singing Games)

A pares y nones ▶

Evens and Odds

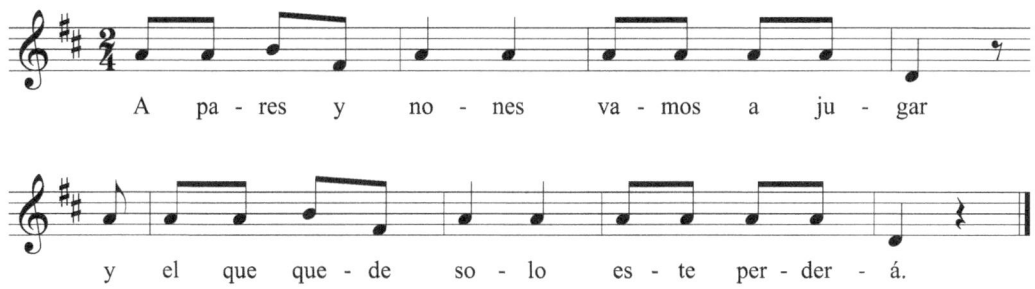

A pa - res y no - nes va - mos a ju - gar
y el que que - de so - lo es - te per - der - á.

Formation: Standing circle holding hands with a leader as part of the circle

Directions: The children sing while walking in the circle holding hands. At the end of the song they stop, and the leader calls out a number, for example, *tres* (three). The children must quickly form groups of three and those left out are eliminated from the game. The singing game is repeated until there are two children left, who are the winners.

Translation:
Evens and odds let's play
and whoever is left alone will lose.

Source: Children at Escuela Pablo Antonio Cuadra (Granada, Nicaragua)

La Música (The Music)

Campanita de oro

Little Gold Bell

Cam - pa - ni - ta de o - ro, dé - ja - me pa - sar

con to - dos mis hi - jos me - nos los de a - trás.

¡Se - rá san - dí - a, se - rá me - lón, se - rá tu pa - pá, se - rá pe - lón!

Formation: Two children face each other with hands clasped and raised to form a bridge. The other children form a single line behind a leader.

Directions: The two children forming the bridge secretly decide who represents *sandía* (watermelon) and who represents *melón* (melon). The children sing while the line leader leads them freely about the space passing under the bridge as desired. When the word *pelón* is chanted, the children forming the bridge lower their arms to catch someone. They ask that child, "*¿Qué quieres, sandía o melón?*" (What do you want, watermelon or melon?). The child whispers a response and then is told to stand directly behind the one who represents their choice. The singing game is repeated until everyone is lined up. The two lines then engage in a tug-of-war.

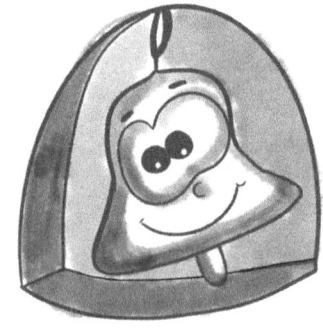

Translation:
Little gold bell let me pass
with all my children except those in the back.
It will be watermelon, it will be melon, it will be your father, he will be bald!

Source: María Carmelina Ajcalón, Nicolasa Peréz, and Florinda García (Panajachel, Guatemala)

This popular singing game of Spanish origin is the B section in "Nerón, Néron" from Nicaragua (in this collection) and the C section in "La víbora de la mar" from Mexico, which demonstrates that these variants have been shaped over time and locations.

Doña Ana

Doña Ana

Do - ña An - a no_es - tá_a - quí, an - da_en su ver - gel a - bri - en - do la ro - sa y_ce - rran - do el cla - vel.

Formation: Standing circle holding hands with a leader in the middle

Directions: The children sing while walking in the circle holding hands. At the end of the song they stop and ask, "*¿Ahí está Doña Ana?*" (Is Doña Ana there?). The leader may improvise a response, for example: "*No, ella está leyendo*" (No, she is reading) or "*No, ella está cantando*" (No, she is singing). After an improvised response, the children walk, sing, and ask the question again. The leader may improvise an answer again, but if they respond "*¡No, ella se murió!*" (No, she died!) the children scatter while the leader tries to tag someone. The child that is tagged becomes the new leader and the singing game is repeated.

Translation: Doña Ana is not here, she walks in her orchard, opening the rose and closing the carnation.

Sources: Isabel Águirre and children at Escuela La Amistad (Masaya, Nicaragua), children at Escuela Pablo Antonio Cuadra (Granada, Nicaragua), teachers at La Mariposa Spanish School (San Juan de la Concepción), La Familia Paéz (Granada, Nicaragua)

Doña Ana is a very popular singing game in Nicaragua with roots traced to the 1200s in Spain. Multiple variants exist throughout Hispanic countries, each with different rhythmic, melodic, and lyrical content.

La Música (The Music)

El caracolito

The Little Snail

Formation: Standing line holding hands with leader 1 at one end and leader 2 at the other end

Directions:

mm. 1–7: The children sing while leader 1 walks and spins to wind the line into a spiral. These measures can be repeated until the spiral is complete.

mm. 8–16: The children sing while leader 2 walks to unwind the spiral. These measures can be repeated until the spiral is unwound.

Translation:

In the sea I saw, in the sea I saw
a snail wind up like this.
The next day in the sea I saw
the snail unwind like this.

Source: Luz Adriana Cutillo Mogollón and children at Escuela Modelo Inclusiva de Educación (Panajachel, Guatemala)

Rondas (Singing Games)

El patio de mi casa (Guatemala)

My Backyard

La Música (The Music)

Formation: Standing circle holding hands with a leader in the middle

Directions: The children sing while engaging in the following actions:
mm. 1–8: Walk in the circle
m. 9: Crouch down low
m. 10: Stand up
m. 11: Crouch down low
m. 12: Stand up
mm. 13–14: Walk in the circle
m. 15: Crouch down low
mm. 17–20: Walk toward the center of the circle
mm. 21–24: Walk backward to form the larger circle

Translation:
My backyard is special,
it gets wet and dries like all the rest.
Crouch down and crouch down again,
beautiful children know how to crouch.
Chocolate, grinder,
stretch, stretch, the queen will pass by.

Sources: María Carmelina Ajcalón (Panajachel, Guatemala), Merlyn Rubí Celada García and children at Escuela Modelo Inclusiva de Educación (Panajachel, Guatemala)

Traced to the 1800s in Spain, this singing game has traveled to other Hispanic countries. Several variants were observed in both Guatemala and Nicaragua.

El patio de mi casa (Nicaragua)

My Backyard

El pa - tio de mi ca - sa es par - ti - cu - lar,

cuan - do llue - ve se mo - ja co - mo los de - más.

A - gá - cha - té y vuel - va te_a - ga - char

que los a - ga - cha - di — tos se sa — ben ju - gar.

Ha - che, i, jo - ta, ka, e - le, e - me, e - ne, a, o,

que si tú no me quie - res o - tro_a - mi - go me que - rrá.
 ten - dré yo

Cho - co - la - te, mo - li - ni - llo, co - rre, co - rre, que te pi -

llo, es - ti - rar, es - ti - rar, que la rei - na va_a pa - sar.

La Música (The Music)

Formation: Standing circle with a leader as part of the circle

Directions:
mm. 1–8: Skip in the circle
(*mm. 4–6:* Raise hands and mimic falling rain)
m. 9: Stop and crouch down low
m. 11: Crouch down lower
mm. 13–16: Rise up while dancing
mm. 17–25: Skip in the circle (reverse direction for repeat)
mm. 25–28: Stop and mimic stirring pot of chocolate
mm. 29–30: Run in place
mm. 31–32: Pretend tag the child to your right
mm. 33–37: The circle moves together to form two lines with the leader at one end. Children across from each other hold hands and raise them to form bridges. The leader runs underneath the long bridge.

Translation:
My backyard is special,
it gets wet and dries like all the rest.
Crouch down and crouch down again
the children who crouched down know how to play.
H, I, J, K, L, M, N, A,
If you don't love me another one will.
H, I, J, K, L, M, N, O,
If you don't love me I will have another friend.
Chocolate, grinder, run, run, or I'll catch you,
stretch, stretch, the queen will pass by.

Source: Teachers at La Mariposa Spanish School (San Juan de la Concepción, Nicaragua)

In the courtyard of the school surrounded by lush greenery, the teachers engaged in a lively demonstration of this traditional singing game. Different in text, form, and game than the Guatemalan variant, it is similar to a version played in Puerto Rico.

El toro toronjil

The Toronjil Bull

Va - mos a la vuel - ta del to - ro, to - ron - jil
a ver a la ra - na co - mien - do pe - re - jil.
La ra - na no_es - tá a - quí es - ta - rá en su ver - gel
cor - tan - do u - na ro - sa, sem - bran - do un cla - vel.

Formation: Standing circle holding hands with *la ranita* (the little frog) in the middle

Directions: The children sing while skipping in the circle around *la ranita*. At the end of the song, they stop and ask, "*Como está la ranita?*" (How is the little frog?). *La ranita* may improvise a response, for example: "*Estoy feliz*" (I am happy) or "*Estoy triste*" (I am sad). After an improvised response, the children skip, sing, and ask the question again. *La ranita* may improvise an answer again, but if they respond, "*¡Engusanada!*" (Full of worms!) the children scatter while *la ranita* tries to tag someone. The child that is tagged becomes *la ranita* and the singing game is repeated.

Translation:
Let's go around the toronjil bull
to see the frog eating parsley.
The frog is not here he will be in his garden
cutting a rose and planting a carnation.

Source: La Familia Ical (Panajachel, Guatemala)

With origins in Spain, this singing game has many variants.

La Música (The Music)

Juguemos en el bosque

Let's Play in the Forest

Ju - gue - mos en el bos - que mien - tras el lo - bo no es - tá.
Si el lo - bo a - pa - re - ce a to - dos nos co - me - rá.

Formation: Standing circle holding hands with *el lobo* (the wolf) on the outside

Directions: The children sing while walking in the circle holding hands. At the end of the song they stop and ask, "¿*Lobo, lobo estás allí?*" (Wolf, wolf, are you there?). *El lobo* responds, "*¡Sí!*" (Yes!). The group then asks, "¿*Que estás haciendo?*" (What are you doing?). *El lobo* may improvise a response, for example: "*Estoy cocinando*" (I am cooking.) or "*Estoy durmiendo.*" (I am sleeping.). After an improvised response, the children walk, sing, and ask the question again. *El lobo* may improvise an answer again, but if they say, "*¡Estoy listo/a* para comer!*" (I am ready to eat!) the children scatter while *el lobo* tries to tag as many children as they can. The children who are tagged become wolves (chasers) and join *el lobo* outside the circle for the next repetition. The game is repeated until all of the children have been tagged.

*listo (masculine), lista (feminine). To make this gender neutral, *el lobo* may respond, "*¡Tengo hambre!*" (I am hungry!).

Translation:
Let's play in the forest while the wolf is not here.
If the wolf appears he will eat us all.

Source: María Carmelina Ajcalón (Panajachel, Guatemala)

This popular singing game is enjoyed in several countries, including the United States, Canada, Greece, and Mexico.

La pájara pinta (variant 1)

The Painted Bird

Formation: Standing circle holding hands with *la pájara pinta* (the painted bird) in the middle

Directions: The children sing while *la pájara pinta* skips around the inside of the circle and stops at the nearest child on the syllable *-món* (*m. 8*). That child gets down on one knee (*m. 11*) and pleads for forgiveness to *la pájara pinta* (*m. 15*) who then waves goodbye to the child.

Game ending variants:

1. The kneeling child switches places with the leader and the game is repeated.
2. The kneeling child leaves the circle and is given a task by the leader, for example, jump up and down ten times. In the music classroom, the eliminated children can choose an instrument and create a rhythmic or melodic accompaniment. The singing game is repeated until there is one child left, who is the winner.

La Música (The Music)

Translation:
The painted bird is already sitting on a lemon tree,
with its wings it collects flowers, with its beak it collects the lemon.
Ay, ay, ay, kneel down,
Ay, ay, ay, ask for forgiveness.

Source: Teachers at La Mariposa Spanish School (San Juan de la Concepción, Nicaragua)

The singing game has origins in Spain with known variants in Argentina, Uruguay, Venezuela, Ecuador, Mexico, Puerto Rico, Dominican Republic, Nicaragua, and most likely other locations. It is cited that *la pajara pinta*, historically played by a girl, is independent and free to fly away from a partner at her own free will, thus communicating a theme of female strength and independence.

La pájara pinta (variant 2)

The Painted Bird

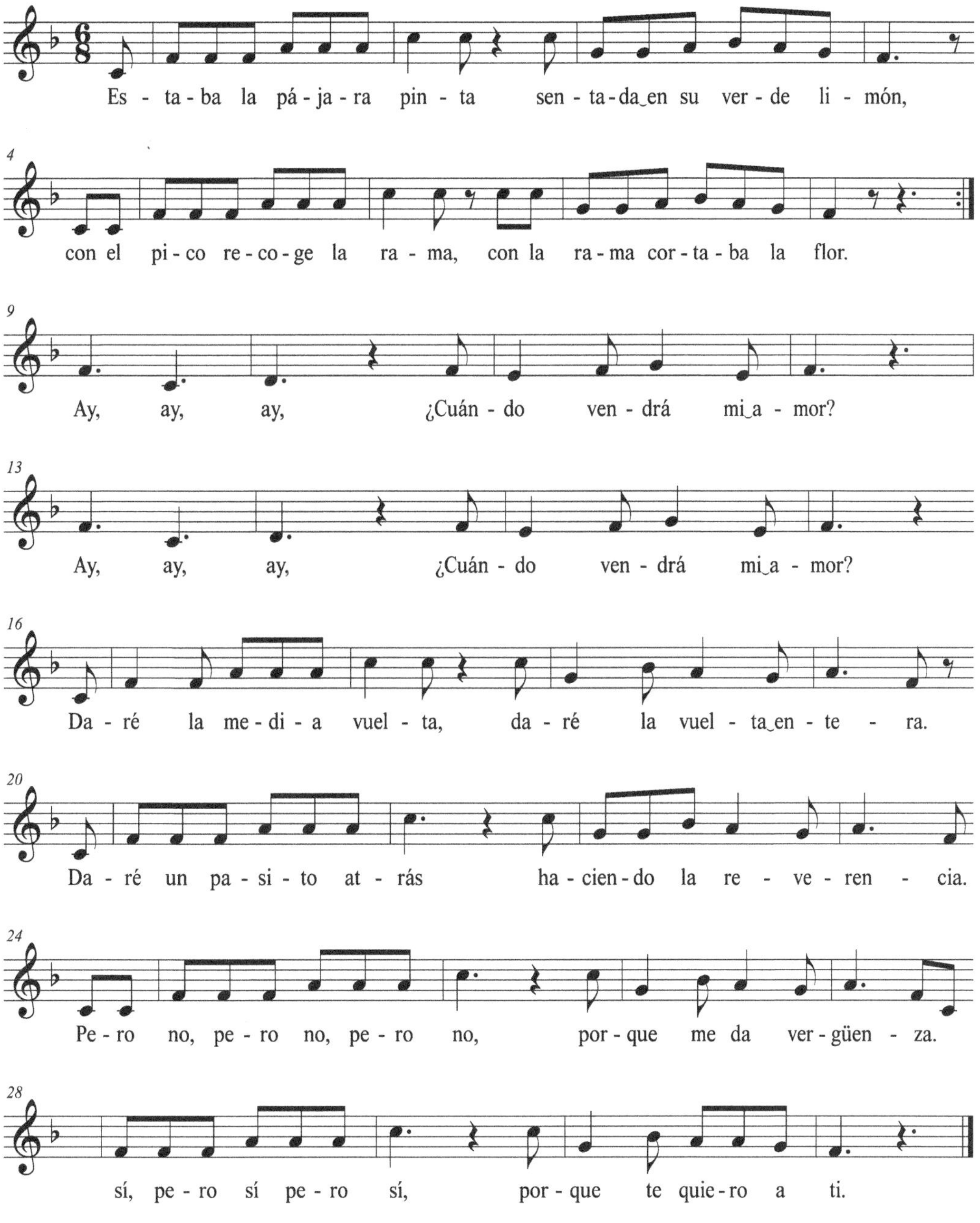

Es - ta - ba la pá - ja - ra pin - ta sen - ta - da en su ver - de li - món,

con el pi - co re - co - ge la ra - ma, con la ra - ma cor - ta - ba la flor.

Ay, ay, ay, ¿Cuán - do ven - drá mi a - mor?

Ay, ay, ay, ¿Cuán - do ven - drá mi a - mor?

Da - ré la me - di - a vuel - ta, da - ré la vuel - ta en - te - ra.

Da - ré un pa - si - to a - trás ha - cien - do la re - ve - ren - cia.

Pe - ro no, pe - ro no, pe - ro no, por - que me da ver - güen - za.

sí, pe - ro sí pe - ro sí, por - que te quie - ro a ti.

La Música (The Music)

Formation: Partners in concentric circles. Each child in the outer circle is facing their partner in the inner circle. Each circle (inside and outside) hold hands.

Directions:

mm. 1–16: Each circle travels to the right (opposite directions) until the players meet back up with their partners.
mm. 17–18: Perform a half turn, partners are now back-to-back
mm. 19–20: Complete the turn, partners are now facing each other
mm. 21–22: Step one foot behind
mm. 23–24: With foot behind, bow to partner
mm. 25–26: Shake head "no"
mm. 27–28: Act embarrassed
mm. 29–31: Shake right hands and hold through *m. 32*
mm. 31–32: Shake left hands and hold

Partners wave goodbye to each other and the inside circle moves to the right to stand in front of a new partner and the singing game is repeated.

Source: Teachers at La Mariposa Spanish School (San Juan de la Concepción, Nicaragua)

Nerón, Nerón

Nerón, Nerón

Ne - rón, Ne - rón, ¿dón - de pa - sa tan - ta gen - te?
la Ca - lle San Vi - cen - te, que pa - sa el rey, ha de pa - sar.
El hi - jo del Con - de se que - da
a - trás, a - trás, a - trás, a - trás, a - trás.
Cam - pa - ni - ta de o - ro, dé - ja - me pa - sar
con to - dos mis hi - ji - tos me - nos el de a - trás.

Formation: Two children face each other with hands clasped and raised to form a bridge. The other children form a single line behind a leader.

Directions: The two children forming the bridge secretly decide who represents *el Sol* (the sun) and who represents *la Luna* (the moon). The children sing while the line leader walks freely about the space passing under the bridge as desired. When the syllable -*trás* is sung, the children forming the bridge lower their arms to catch someone (*m. 15*), gently tosses them back and forth (*mm. 16–23*), and at the end of the song asks them, "*¿Qué quieres, el Sol o la Luna?*" (What do you want, the Sun or the Moon?). The child whispers a response and then is told to stand directly behind the one who represents their choice. The singing game is repeated until everyone is lined up. The two lines then engage in a tug-of-war.

La Música (The Music)

Translation:
Nerón, Nerón, where do so many people go?
San Vicente Street, let the King through, he has to go through.
The son of the Count stays behind, behind, behind, behind, behind.
Little golden bell, let me go by
with all of my little children except the one in back.

Source: Teachers at La Mariposa Spanish School (San Juan de la Concepción, Nicaragua)

With origins in Spain, this singing game is claimed to reaffirm notions of good and bad as represented by *el Sol* (the Sun) and *la Luna* (the Moon). Asalia led the groups of teachers in a very energetic performance of this traditional singing game from their childhood. The tug-of-war at the end was with a human chain as they wrapped their arms around each other's waists and pulled.

Pollos y pollitos

Chickens and Chicks

Po - llos y po - lli - tos va - mos a ju - gar,
el po - llo que yo_a - tra - pe e - se per - der - á.

Formation: Two children face each other approximately four feet apart to form a passageway. The other children form a single line of *pollos* (chickens) behind a leader.

Directions: The children sing while the line leader leads them freely about the space and through the passageway as desired. At the end of the song, the two children forming the passageway compete to grab the child closest to them. The child who is caught stands directly behind the one who caught them. The singing game is repeated until all of the children are lined up. The two lines then engage in a tug-of-war.

Translation:
Chickens and chicks let's play,
the chicken that I catch is the loser.

Source: Nicolasa Pérez (Panajachel, Guatemala)

La Música (The Music)

Que llueva

Let It Rain

Que llue-va, que llue-va, el quet-zal de la cue-va,
que llue-va, que llue-va, el quet-zal de la cue-va,
los pa-ja-ri-tos can - tan, las nu-bes se le-van - tan.
¡Que sí! ¡Que no! ¡Que cai-ga un cha-pa-rrón!
¡Que sí! ¡Que no! ¡Que cai-ga un cha-pa-rrón!

Formation: Standing circle with a leader in the middle

Directions: The children sing and chant while the leader skips around the inside of the circle. At the end of the chant, the leader calls on someone by stating a physical characteristic, for example, "*Le cae la persona con <u>la camisa verde</u>*" (Out goes the person with <u>the green shirt</u>).

Game ending variants:

1. The child with the green shirt switches places with the leader and the singing game is repeated.
2. The child with the green shirt leaves the circle and the singing game is repeated until there is one child left, who is the winner.

Translation:
Let it rain, let it rain, the quetzal is in the cave,
let it rain, let it rain, the quetzal is in the cave,
the birds sing, the clouds rise.
Yes! No! Let there be a downpour!
Yes! No! Let there be a downpour!

Sources: María Carmelina Ajcalón (Panajachel, Guatemala), Teachers at La Mariposa Spanish School (San Juan de la Concepción, Nicaragua), La Familia Páez (Granada, Nicaragua)

The traditional first line is "*Que llueva, que llueva, la virgen de la cueva*" (Let it rain, let it rain, the virgin of the cave). One legend claims that the cave referenced is located in La Villa de Altura in Valencia, Spain, where inside there is a chapel of Virgin Mary. In 1726 the community experienced a severe drought that jeopardized the crops and the farmers prayed to *La Virgen de la cueva* (the Virgin of the cave) for rain. The next day they welcomed a downpour. It is believed that the singing game is based on these events.

Carmelina changes the traditional lyrics and sings "*quetzal*" (national bird of Guatemala) instead of "*virgen*." She commented that this is fairly common when singing with children, and upon each repetition she or a child would choose a different animal.

La Música (The Music)

Ronda de la mano

Hand Circle Game

Translation:

Give me one hand, give me the other, let's make a big circle.
Give me one hand, give me the other, let's make a big circle.
A little circle, a big circle,
a tall circle, a short circle,
a jumping circle, a circle on one foot,
a sitting circle, because I got tired.

Formation: Standing circle holding hands

Directions: The children sing while engaging in the following actions:

mm. 1–8: Walk in the circle holding hands

mm. 9–10: Walk toward the center of the circle

mm. 11–12: Walk backward to form the larger circle

mm. 13–14: Raise hands up high

mm. 15–16: Crouch down low

mm. 17–18: Jump in place

mm. 19–20: Jump in place on one foot

mm. 21–24: Sit down in the circle

Source: La Familia Ical (Panajachel, Guatemala)

This lovely circle game allows the children to kinesthetically experience opposites: large/small and tall/short.

La Música (The Music)

Ronda el campanario

Around the Bell Tower

Formation: Partners in concentric circles. Each child in the outer circle faces their partner in the inner circle.

Directions:

mm. 2–3: Clap hands as indicated

mm. 5–6: Stomp feet as indicated

mm. 7–10: Two-hand turn with partner

mm. 11–12: Shake right hand with partner

mm. 13–14: Shake left hand with partner

mm. 15–18: Children in the inside circle spin and travel counterclockwise to meet up with the next child in the outer circle, who becomes their new partner.

The singing game is repeated until the children are back with their original partners.

Translation:
They clap well and with feet, too
around the bell tower again.
Greetings over here, greetings over there,
around the bell tower again.

Source: La Familia González (Panajachel, Guatemala)

Our homestay family taught us this singing game. It is unique to this collection as it is the only song written with a *la tetratonic* scale.

La Música (The Music)

Rueda, rueda

Around and Around

Rue - da, rue - da, rue - da, a - rri - ba la ca - fe - te - ra,
a - ba - jo la a-zu - ca - re - ra, me gus-ta la-var la ro - pa,
me gus-ta ser e - le - gan - te, tam - po-co con e - le - fan - te.
Pi - ña, na - ran - ja, li - món, que cai - ga el vie-jo pan - zón.

Formation: Standing circle with a leader in the middle

Directions: The children sing while engaging in the following actions:

mm. 1–2: Skip in the circle

mm. 3–4: Stop and raise hands up high

mm. 5–6: Reach hands down low

mm. 7–8: Act out washing a piece of clothing on leg as if it is a washboard

mm. 9–10: Touch clothing

mm. 11–12: Mimic an elephant's trunk

mm. 13–16: Leader points to each child around the circle on the steady beat and stops on the syllable *-zón*.

Game ending variants:

1. The child that the leader is pointing to switches places with the leader and the singing game is repeated.
2. The child that the leader is pointing to leaves the circle and the singing game is repeated until there is one child left, who then chases all of the children to try and tag someone.

Translation:
Around and around, above the coffee maker,
below the sugar bowl, I like to wash the clothes,
I like to be elegant, not with the elephant.
Pineapple, orange, lemon, may the old pot-bellied guy fall.

Sources: Teachers at La Mariposa Spanish School (San Juan de la Concepción, Nicaragua), La Familia Páez (Granada, Nicaragua)

Variants of this popular singing game can be witnessed in El Salvador, Colombia, Uruguay, and other Hispanic countries. With a large group of teachers, Asalia led a vibrant demonstration of a favorite childhood game.

La Música (The Music)

Salí, tortúga

Come Out, Turtle

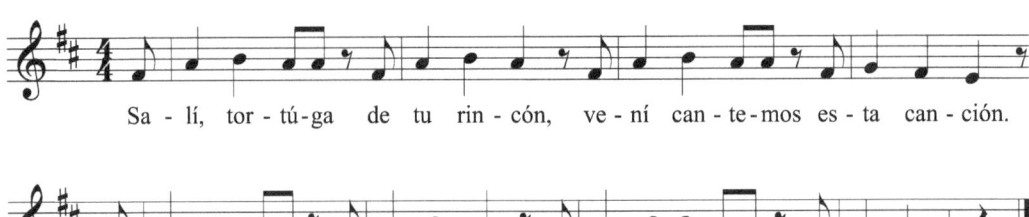

Sa - lí, tor - tú - ga de tu rin - cón, ve - ní can - te - mos es - ta can - ción.

Que to - dos sa - ben y yo tam - bién, ca - che - te in - fla - do se - rá us - ted.

Formation: Standing circle holding hands with *la tortuga* (the turtle) in the middle

Directions: The children sing, walking in the circle while *la tortuga* dances in the middle. *La tortuga* points to three consecutive children on the last syllables *-rá us - ted* and that third child becomes the *la tortuga* and the singing game is repeated.

Translation:
Turtle, come out from your corner, come, let's sing this song.
Everyone knows and me too, chubby cheeks you will have.

Source: Isabel Águirre and children at La Amistad Escuela (Masaya, Nicaragua)

Soy una serpiente

I Am a Snake

Formation: Standing or sitting circle with *el serpiente* (the snake) in the middle

Directions: The children sing while *el serpiente* walks freely about the space. At the end of the song, *el serpiente* stops and asks a child, "*¿Quiere ser usted una parte de mi cola?*" (Do you want to be a part of my tail?). The child responds, "*¡Sí!*" and crawls through the snake's spread-apart legs and then places their hands on *el serpiente's* waist or shoulders from behind to form a part of the snake's tail. The singing game is repeated until each child is a part of the tail. During each repetition, *el serpiente* may change the singing and walking tempo and the snake tail follows.

Translation:
I am a snake that walks through the forest
looking for a part of my tail.
Do you want to be a part of my tail?

Sources: Luz Adriana Cutillo Mogollón and children at Escuela Modelo Inclusiva de Educación (Panajachel, Guatemala), Teachers at La Mariposa Spanish School (San Juan de la Concepción, Nicaragua)

This game has origins in Europe and has been in practice in youth camps and physical education classes in Central and South America.

Rimas y juegos
Rhymes and Games

Abuelita de Perú

Grandma from Peru

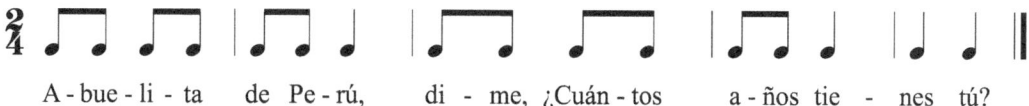

A - bue - li - ta   de Pe - rú,   di - me, ¿Cuán - tos   a - ños tie - nes tú?

Formation: Standing circle with one foot forward and a leader in the middle

Directions: The leader chants while pointing to each foot around the circle on the steady beat and stops on the last word, *tú*. The leader asks that child, "*¿Cuantos años tienes?*" (How old are you?). The child states their age, for example, *siete* (seven), and the leader then counts to seven in Spanish while continuing to point to each foot around the circle and stops on the number seven. The child that the leader is pointing to leaves the circle. The game is repeated until there is one child remaining who chases the group to tag someone.

Game ending variants:

1. The child who is tagged becomes the new leader and the game is repeated.
2. Each child who is tagged immediately becomes a chaser and the game ends after everyone has been tagged.

Translation:
Grandmother from Peru, tell me, how old are you?

Source: Teachers at La Mariposa Spanish School (San Juan de la Concepción, Nicaragua)

The teachers played this energetic game in the school's nature reserve. It is well loved and has been observed on playgrounds in many Hispanic countries as a counting-out rhyme, jump-rope game, or with a paper fortune teller. The variant "Zapatito Cochinito" was played by children at Escuela La Amistad (Masaya, Nicaragua) and "Manzanita de Perú" is played in Perú.

La Música (The Music)

Bate, bate chocolate

Stir, Stir the Chocolate

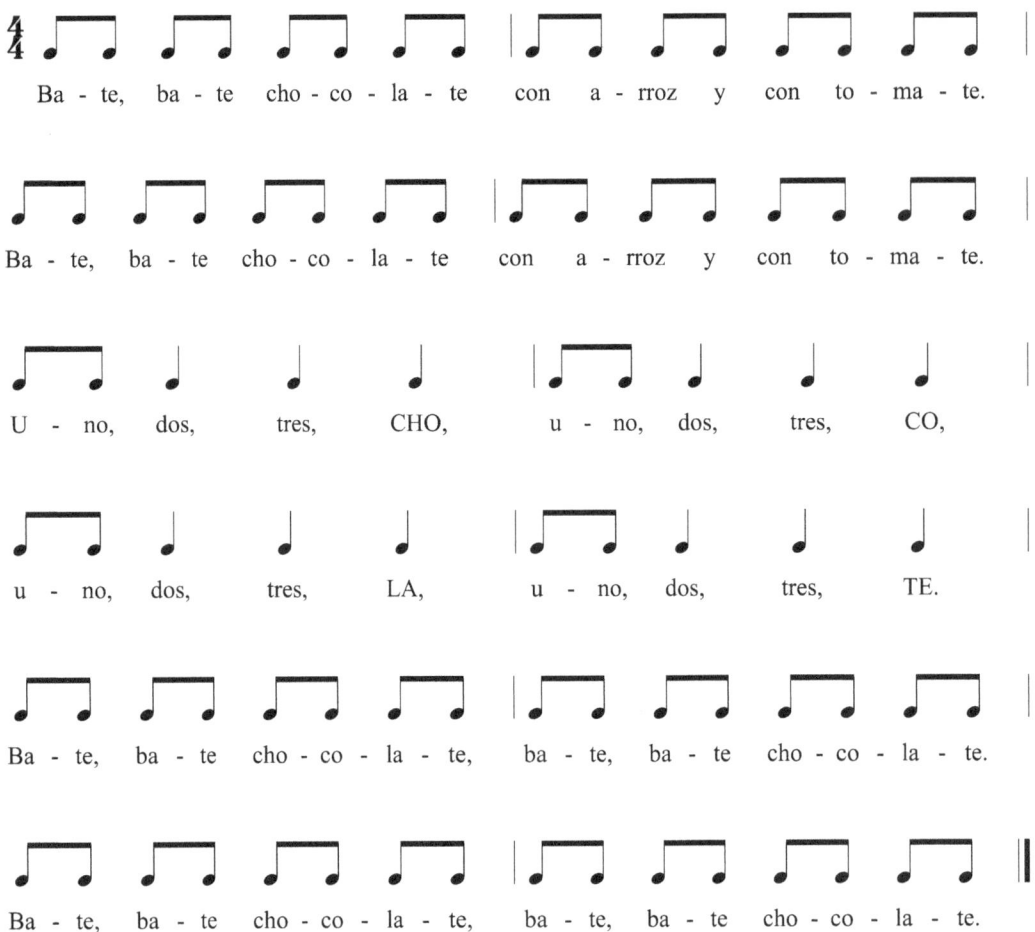

Translation:
Stir, stir the chocolate with rice and tomato.
Stir, stir the chocolate with rice and tomato.
One, two, three, CHO, one, two, three, CO,
one, two, three, LA, one, two, three, TE.
Stir, stir the chocolate, stir, stir the chocolate.
Stir, stir the chocolate, stir, stir the chocolate.

Source: Children at Escuela Pablo Antonio Cuadra (Granada, Nicaragua)

Caracol ▶
Snail

Aquel caracol
que va por el sol
en cada ramita
llevaba una flor

Qué viva la gracia
qué viva el amor
qué viva la gracia
de aquel caracol

Translation:
That snail
that goes by the sun
on each twig
carrying a flower

Long live grace
long live love
long live grace
of that snail

Source: Children at Escuela República de Cuba (San Juan de la Concepción, Nicaragua)

A first-grade class recited this popular poem with spontaneous accompanying actions. It is very common for Nicaraguan children to recite poetry in families and schools as inspired by the poet Rubén Darío (1867–1916). A national treasure, he is recognized for initiating the Spanish-American literary movement, *modernismo*.

La Música (The Music)

Chocolate

Chocolate

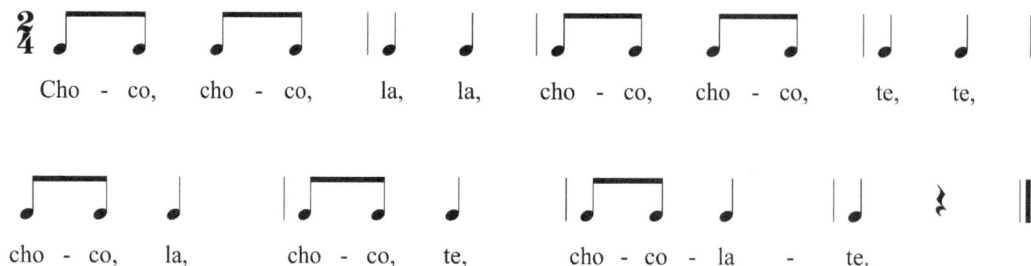

Cho - co, cho - co, la, la, cho - co, cho - co, te, te, cho - co, la, cho - co, te, cho - co - la - te.

Formation: Partners facing each other

Directions: While chanting, engage in the following actions on the steady beat and aligned with the text:

choco: clap partner's hands
la: clap back of partner's hands
te: bump fists with partner

Source: Children at Escuela Pablo Antonio Cuadra (Granada, Nicaragua)

Chocolate dates back to the Olmec and Mayan civilizations. It is made from the fruit of cacao trees and was used as a form of unsweetened spice and to create highly revered drinks.

Rimas y Juegos (Rhymes and Games)

¿Cuántos años tiene la niña?
How Old is the Girl?

¿Cuán - tos a - ños ti - e - ne la ni - ña? La ni - ña ti - e - ne
u - no, dos, tres, cua - tro, cin - co, seis.....

Material: Long jump rope

Formation: Two rope turners and one jumper

Directions: The turners chant while one child jumps rope. The turners continue chanting numbers until the jumper falters.

Translation:
How old is the girl? The girl is
one, two, three, four, five six . . .

Source: Children at Escuela Pablo Antonio Cuadra (Granada, Nicaragua)

Jump-rope rhymes were common on this school playground, especially with the first-, second-, and third-grade girls.

La Música (The Music)

El baile de la gallina

The Chicken Dance

Yo quie - ro bai - lar. Yo quie - ro bai - lar.
El bai - le la ga - lli - na, yo quie - ro bai - lar.
A - li - ta por a - quí, a - li - ta por a - llá,
pe - chi - to por de - lan - te, co - li - ta por de - trás.

Queremos bailar. Queremos bailar.
El baile la gallina, queremos bailar . . .

Directions:

mm. 1–4: Clap the steady beat and dance
m. 5: Flap one *wing* (arm bent, elbow out)
m. 6: Flap the other *wing*
m. 7: Chest extended forward
m. 8: Wag *tail* back and forth

Translation:

I want to dance. I want to dance.
The chicken dance, I want to dance.
Little wing over here, little wing over there,
little chest in front, little tail behind.

We want to dance. We want to dance.

Source: Isabel Águirre and children at Escuela La Amistad (Masaya, Nicaragua)

Rimas y Juegos (Rhymes and Games)

El barco se hunde ▶

The Ship Sinks

El bar - co se hun - de, se hun - de,
vie - nen las o - las, gru - pos de *tres*.

Formation: Standing circle holding hands with a leader as part of the circle

Directions: The children chant while walking in the circle holding hands. At the end of the chant, they stop and the leader calls out a number, for example, *seis* (six). The children must quickly form groups of six and those left out are eliminated from the game. Repeat until there are two children left, who are the winners.

Translation:
The boat sinks, sinks,
the waves come, groups of *six*.

Source: Children at Escuela Pablo Antonio Cuadra (Granada, Nicaragua)

A lively elimination game, a group of fourth graders played this often during recess with laughter, negotiations, and joy.

La Música (The Music)

El florón

The Flower

El flo-rón es-tá en la ma-no, en la ma-no es-tá el flo-rón,
flo-ren-ci-to de mi vi-da, flo-rón de mi co-ra-zón.
Por a-quí pa-só, por a-llá pa-só, el bien de mi vi-da, ¿En quién que-dó?

Material: A flower, ring, coin, or small object

Formation: Standing or sitting circle with a leader on the inside

Directions: The children place their palms together and the leader holds the small object between their palms. The children chant while the leader taps each child's hands around the circle on the steady beat. The leader secretly drops the small object into the hands of one of the children. The child whose hands were tapped on the last beat of the chant tries to guess who has the object.

Translation:
The flower is in the hand, in the hand is the flower,
little flower of my life, flower of my heart.
It passed here, it passed there, the good in my life, with whom did it stay?

Source: Teacher at La Mariposa Spanish School (San Juan de la Concepción, Nicaragua)

El pájaro sin jaula

The Bird without a Cage

Formation: Groups of three, scattered. In each group, two of the children face each other and hold hands to form *la jaula* (the cage). The third child, *el pájaro* (the bird), stands inside the cage. One child stands alone, a bird without a cage.

Directions: The bird without a cage emits a bird call, which prompts all of the cages to open. (The children forming the cages lift their arms while still holding hands.) The birds fly around the space in search of a new cage, including the bird initially without one. When a bird enters a cage, arms are lowered to close it. There will be one child without a cage again, and the game is repeated.

Source: La Familia Ical (Panajachel, Guatemala)

La Música (The Music)

El pato

The Duck

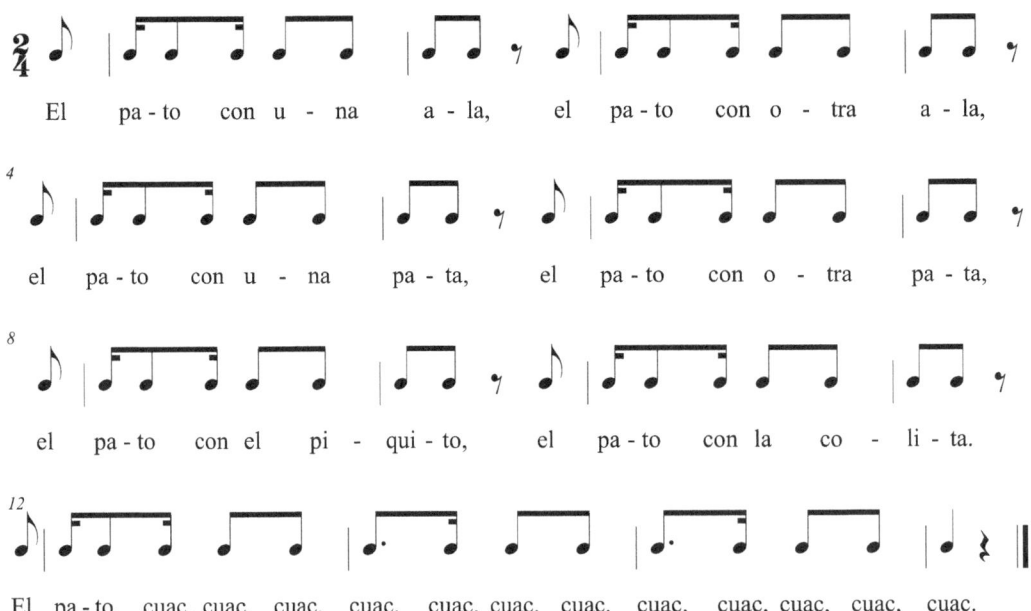

Directions: The children chant while engaging in the following actions:

mm.1–2: Flap one *wing* (arm bent, elbow out)

mm. 3–4: Flap the other *wing*

mm. 5–6: Tap one foot on ground

mm. 7–8: Tap the other foot on ground

mm. 9–10: Open and close *beak* (two hands at mouth)

mm. 11–12: Wag *tail*

mm. 13–15: Flap *wings*, walk in place, and wag *tail*

Translation:

The duck with one wing, the duck with another wing,
the duck with a foot, the duck with another foot,
the duck with a little beak, the duck with a little tail.
Quack, quack, quack, quack . . .

Sources: Damaris Santizo and children at Escuela Modelo Inclusiva de Educación (Panajachel, Guatemala), Ingrid Riquiac (Panajachel, Guatemala)

Rimas y Juegos (Rhymes and Games)

Gallina colorada

Red Hen

U - na ga - lli - na en un a - ra - do pu - so un hue - vo co - lo - ra - do.

Chanted: Puso uno, puso dos, puso tres, puso cuatro . . .

Directions: The children sing and then chant, "*Puso <u>uno</u>, puso <u>dos</u>, puso <u>tres</u>, puso <u>cuatro</u> . . .*" and continue counting as long as they are able without taking a breath. The one who chants the longest is the winner.

Translation:
A hen in a plow laid a red egg.
Laid one, laid two, laid three, laid four . . .

Source: Lidia Hernández (San Juan de La Concepción, Nicaragua)

In a variant from Spain, "Gallina la pavada," the children sit in a circle with both legs extended. A leader in the center points to each foot on the steady beat stopping on the number eight for each repetition, and that child removes their foot. This continues until there is one foot remaining and that child is the winner.

La Música (The Music)

Muchos pececitos

Many Little Fish

Mu - chos pe - ce - ci - tos que fue - ron a na - dar,
lo más pe - que - ni - to se fue al fon - do del mar.
Vió un ti - bu - rón y le di - jo, "Ven a - cá."
"No, no, no, no, no," me re - ga - ña mi ma - má.

Formation: Standing circle of *pececitos* (little fish) with *el tiburón* (the shark) in the middle

Directions: The children chant with accompanying actions. At the end they scatter while the shark tries to tag someone. The child who is tagged joins the shark in the middle of the circle for the next repetition and the two sharks each try to tag someone. The game is repeated until all of the fish are caught.

mm. 1–6: Palms together, move left and right to mimic a swimming fish
mm. 7–8: Crouch down low, hands on the floor
mm. 9–12: Hands above head, palm-to-palm, to mimic a shark fin
mm. 13–16: Wag finger in a scolding manner

Translation:
Many little fish went swimming,
the littlest one went to the bottom of the sea.
They saw a shark that said, "Come here."
"No, no, no, no, no," my mother scolds me.

Source: Merlyn Rubí Celada García and children at Escuela Modelo Inclusiva de Educación (Panajachel, Guatemala)

Rimas y Juegos (Rhymes and Games)

Periquito el bandolero

The Bandit Parakeet

Formation: Standing circle with a leader in the middle

Directions: The leader chants while pointing to each child around the circle on the steady beat and stops on the last syllable, *-vó*. That child is out and leaves the circle. Repeat until there is one child left, who is the winner.

Translation:
Parakeet the bandit, got into a hat.
The hat was straw, he got into a box.
The box was made of cardboard, he got into a cucumber.
The cucumber ripened and the parakeet was saved.

Source: Children at Escuela Pablo Antonio Cuadra (Granada, Nicaragua)

La Música (The Music)

Pikachú

Picachu

Pi - ka - chú, pi - ca por a - rri - ba, pi - ca por a - ba - jo, pi - ka - chú, pi - ka - chú.

Formation: Partners facing each other

Hand-clapping Pattern: On the steady beat
Beat 1: Palms together, move hands to the left to swipe back of hands
Beat 2: Palms together, move hands to the right to swipe back of hands
Beat 3: Palms together, move hands to the left to clap and hold back of hands
Beat 4: Right hands clap own left hands
Beat 5: Right hands clap above left hands
Beat 6: Right hands clap own left hands
Beat 7: Right hands clap below left hands
Beats 8-9: Shake right fist
Beat 10: With right hand, choose "rock," "paper," or "scissors"
Repeat *beats 8–10* if there is a tie.

The winner of rock, paper, scissors pinches their partner's cheek. While still pinching the cheek, *beats 8–10* are repeated until one child is pinching both cheeks and they are the winner.

Translation:
Pikachu, touch from above, touch from below,
pikachu, pikachu.

Source: Child and school volunteer at Escuela Pablo Antonio Cuadra (Granada, Nicaragua)

This hand-clapping game is played in several world cultures and demonstrates the integration of popular culture into children's rhymes.

¿Quién se comió el pastel?

Who Ate the Cake?

Ro - sa se co - mió el pas - tel que lo hi - zo su ma - má.

¿Quién yo? ¡Sí, us - ted! ¡Yo no fuí! ¿Quién fue? ¡Fue Pa-blo!

Formation: Sitting circle

Directions: The children chant and the one who is called on (Rosa) chants their responses and then chooses a new child (Pablo). The game is repeated, substituting Pablo for Rosa. Repeat as many times as desired, eventually calling on all of the children in the circle.

Translation:
Rosa ate the cake that her mother made.
Who me? Yes, you! *It wasn't me!* Then who? *It was Pablo!*

Source: Isabel Águirre and children at La Amistad Escuela (Masaya, Nicaragua)

Isabel and the children engaged in this Spanish language variant of "Who Stole the Cookie from the Cookie Jar?"

La Música (The Music)

Sana, sana

Heal, Heal

Sa - na, sa - na, co - li - ta de ra - na,
si no sa - nas hoy, sa - na - rás ma - ña - na.

Directions: This chant is used to console a child. For example, a father might share this with their child who is hurt or not feeling well.

Translation:
Heal, heal, little frog tail,
if you do not heal today, you will heal tomorrow.

Source: Lidia Hernández (San Juan de la Concepción, Nicaragua)

This chant is common across many Hispanic regions and offers a message of encouragement and healing. If you are suffering today, things will get better tomorrow.

Rimas y Juegos (Rhymes and Games)

Señor Lobo ▶

Mr. Wolf

Formation: Standing line, shoulder-to-shoulder, facing Señor Lobo (Mr. Wolf), who is across the field or room.

Directions: The children chant, "*Señor Lobo, Señor Lobo, ¿Qué hora es?*" (Mr. Wolf, Mr. Wolf, What time is it?). Señor Lobo replies with a time, for example, "*Son las tres*" (It is three o'clock). The children then take three steps toward the wolf. The children repeat the question and the wolf may offer a different reply, for example, "*Son las cinco*" (It is five o'clock) and the children take five steps toward the wolf. This is repeated until Señor Lobo replies, "*¡Es la hora de comer!*" (It is time to eat!). The children run while Señor Lobo tries to tag one of them. The tagged child becomes the next Señor Lobo and the game is repeated.

Source: María Carmelina Ajcalón (Panajachel, Guatemala)

Variants of this chasing game are played in many regions of the world including North America, Europe, Caribbean, New Zealand, and South Africa.

La Música (The Music)

Su, su, su

Su, Su, Su

Su, su, su, de la ju-ven-tud, te a-com-pa-ña-ré en cual-quier lu-gar, con la Pep-si, Pep-si, Pep-si, con la Co-la, Co-la, Co-la, con la Pep-si Co-la.

Formation: Partners facing each other

Handclapping Pattern: On the steady beat
Beat 1: Palms together, move hands to the left to swipe back of hands
Beat 2: Palms together, move hands to the right to swipe back of hands
Beat 3: Palms together, move hands to the left to clap and hold back of hands
Beat 4: Right hands clap own left hands
Beat 5: Right hands clap above left hands
Beat 6: Right hands clap own left hands
Beat 7: Right hands clap below left hands
Beat 8: Right hands clap own left hands
  Repeat steps 5–8 two more times.
mm. 9–10: Clap right hands above three times, clap own hand once
mm. 11–12: Clap right hands below three times, clap own hand once
mm. 13–14: Clap right hands above, clap own hand, clap right hands below, try to tickle partner's belly. The one who tickles first, wins.

Translation:
Su, su, su, of youth, I will accompany you anywhere,
with the Pepsi, Pepsi, Pepsi, with the Cola, Cola, Cola, with the Pepsi Cola.

Source: Rosa and Heydi at La Mariposa Spanish School (San Juan de La Concepción, Nicaragua)

Rosa and Heydi provide a very animated rendition of this hand-clapping game. The lyrics demonstrate the integration of popular culture into children's games.

Rimas y Juegos (Rhymes and Games)

Tierra y mar ▶

Land and Sea

Formation: Single file line with a leader apart from the group

Directions: The area on one side of the line represents *tierra* (land) and the other side is *mar* (sea). The leader calls out *tierra* or *mar* and the children must jump sideways to the corresponding side. The leader continues calling and the children must either remain in place or jump to the other side accordingly. If a child makes a mistake they are eliminated from the game. The leader keeps calling until one child is left and they are the winner.

Sources: Children at Escuela Pablo Antonio Cuadra (Granada, Nicaragua), Isabel Águirre and children at La Amistad Escuela (Masaya, Nicaragua)

Jocelyn and her friends engage in this game amid a very bustling playground. They negotiate rules and hold each other accountable, all while maintaining their vibrant children's game culture.

La Música (The Music)

Tortillitas ▶

Little Tortillas

Tor - ti - lli - tas pa - ra ma - má, tor - ti - lli - tas pa - ra pa - pá,
las ga - lle - ti - tas pa - ra ma - má, las do - ra - di - tas pa - ra pa - pá.

Formation: Partners facing each other

Directions: Left hands are placed palm-to-palm and remain in this position for the entire hand-clapping sequence. The following actions are performed with the right hand on the steady beat:

Beat 1: Clap back of partner's left hand
Beat 2: Clap partner's hand above left hands
Beat 3: Clap back of partner's left hand
Beat 4: Clap partner's hand below left hands
Repeat sequence three more times.

At the end of the chant each child tries to tickle their partner's belly. The one who does so first, wins.

Translation:
Little tortillas for mama, little tortillas for papa,
little cookies for mama, little tacos for papa.

Source: Asalia Mercado (San Juan de la Concepción, Nicaragua)

A local lyrical variant of a well-known hand-clapping game, this version uses the word *doraditas* (little tacos), which is the diminutive of *dorados*, a local term for tacos.

Rimas y Juegos (Rhymes and Games)

Va a preparar una ensalada

They are Going to Make a Salad

Va a pre-pa-rar u-na en-sa-la-da, se ne-ce-si-ta.

Chi - le, to - ma - te, li - món, le - chu - ga.

Material: Long jump rope

Formation: Two rope turners and one jumper

Directions: The turners chant while one child jumps rope. The turners repeat the second line until the jumper falters.

Translation:
They are going to prepare a salad, it is needed.
Chile, tomato, lemon, lettuce.

Source: Children at Escuela Pablo Antonio Cuadra (Granada, Nicaragua)

The girls frequently engaged in this jump-rope game during recess. The children opted in and out of several jump-roping groups scattered throughout the schoolyard.

Canciones
Songs

Buenos días

Good Morning

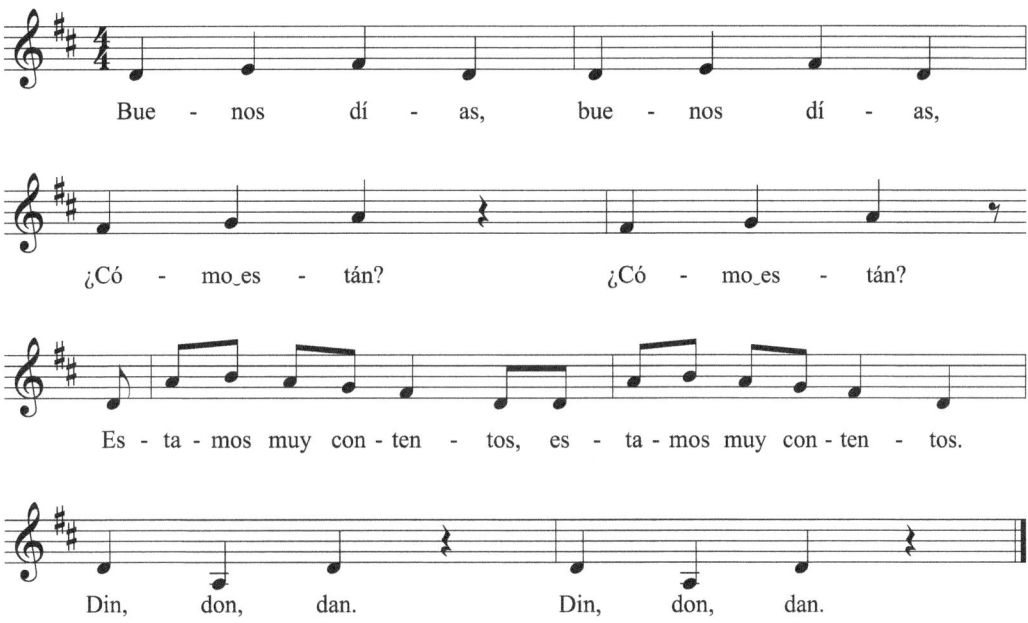

(Buenos días, buenos días,
¿Cómo están? ¿Cómo están?
estamos muy contentos. estamos muy contentos.
Din, don, dan.)

Los colores, los colores
¿Cuáles son? ¿Cuáles son?
Rojo y amarillo, rojo y amarillo,
azul también, azul también.

Nuestra sangre, nuestra sangre,
roja es, roja es.
Ella nos da vida, ella nos da vida,
salud también, salud también.

Translation:
Good morning, good morning,
How are you? How are you?
We are very happy, we are very happy.
Ding, dong, dang. Ding, dong, dang.

The colors, the colors,
What are they? What are they?
Red and yellow, red and yellow,
blue also, blue also.

Our blood, our blood,
is red, is red.
It gives us life, it gives us life,
health also, health also.

La Música (The Music)

Sources: Children at Escuela Pablo Antonio Cuadra (Granada, Nicaragua), Children at Escuela República de Cuba (San Juan de la Concepción, Nicaragua)

Set to the melody of "Frère Jacques," this song was well-loved, very common in elementary schools in Nicaragua, and consistently performed will all three verses.

Buenos días, mi maestra

Good Morning, My Teacher

Translation:
Good morning, my teacher, good morning, come here.
Good morning, little school, that is a temple of knowledge.

Good morning, little friends, we come to study.
Good morning, little friends, study to learn.

Sources: Nora Blass Hernández (San Juan de la Concepción, Nicaragua), Isabel Águirre and children at Escuela La Amistad (Masaya, Nicaragua)

Nora, a retired elementary school teacher, integrated many songs into her classes. She sang this with her young students to begin the school day.

La Música (The Music)

Cabeza, cara, hombros, pies

Head, Face, Shoulders, Feet

Ca - be - za, ca - ra, hom - bros, pies, hom - bros, pies, hom - bros, pies,

ca - be - za, ca - ra, hom - bros, pies y u - na vuel - ta en - te - ra.

Directions:
Touch each body part as it is sung. Turn around once at the end.

Translation:
Head, face, shoulders, feet, shoulders, feet, shoulders, feet,
head, face, shoulders, feet, and a whole turn.

Source: Jocelyn, a fourth-grade student at Escuela Pablo Antonio Cuadra (Granada, Nicaragua)

Jocelyn and a friend shared this song on the playground during recess. She learned many songs from her mother who taught in a nearby preschool.

Canciones (Songs)

Campanero

Bell Ringer

Translation:
Bell ringer, bell ringer,
Where are you? Where are you?
Ring the bell, ring the bell.
Ding, dong, dang. Ding, dong, dang.

Source: La Familia González (Panajachel, Guatemala)

Set to the melody of "Frère Jacques," this Spanish-language variant maintains a similar lyrical translation.

La Música (The Music)

Canto de las vocales

Vowel Song

¡A! La vaca viene ya. ¡E! La vaca ya se fue.
¡I! La vaca ya está aquí. ¡O! La vaca se ahogó.
¡U! La vaca eres tú. La vaca eres tú.

Translation:
A! The cow is coming. E! The cow already left.
I! The cow is already here. O! The cow drowned.
U! The cow is you. The cow is you.

Source: Nora Blass Hernández (San Juan de la Concepción, Nicaragua)

Nora joyfully demonstrated this song, which she sang with her young students to teach vowels.

Caracol ▶

Snail

Ca - ra - col, col, col, sal de tu ca - si - ta,
que es de ma - ña - ni - ta y ha sa - li - do el sol.
Ca - ra - col, col, col, en - tra a tu ca - si - ta,
que es de no - che - ci - ta se ha me - ti - do el sol.

Translation:
Snail, snail, snail, leave your little house,
it is morning and the sun has risen.
Snail, snail, snail, enter your little house,
it is night and the sun has set.

Source: Isabel Águirre and children at La Amistad Escuela (Masaya, Nicaragua)

According to the Mayan legend *El Sol y la Luna*, *el Sol* (the sun) and *la Luna* (the moon) were two gods. *El Sol* was strong but cowardly and *la Luna* was weak but brave. They sacrificed themselves daily to provide light for the world.

La Música (The Music)

Corre, conejito

Run, Little Rabbit

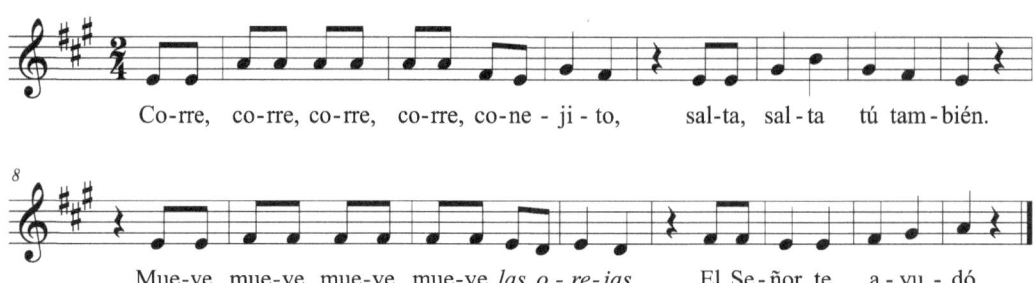

Co-rre, co-rre, co-rre, co-rre, co-ne-ji-to, sal-ta, sal-ta tú tam-bién.

Mue-ve, mue-ve, mue-ve, mue-ve *las o-re-jas,* El Se-ñor te a-yu-dó.

Directions: The children sing while engaging in the following actions:

mm. 1–3: Run in place

mm. 4–7: Jump in place

mm. 8–11: Make rabbit ears with hands and move them

mm. 12–15: Point to sky

For each repetition of the song, change *las orejas* (ears) to another body part, such as *la colita* (little tail) or *las patas* (paws), and move accordingly.

Translation:
Run, run, run, run, little bunny,
jump, jump as well.
Move, move, move, move your ears,
The Lord helped you.

Source: Damaris Santizo and children at Escuela Modelo Inclusiva de Educación (Panajachel, Guatemala)

Religious songs were commonly sung in elementary schools in Guatemala. Damaris shared this lively song with her first-grade students.

Cucú, cucú, cantaba la rana

Cuckoo, Cuckoo, Sang the Frog

(Cucú, cucú, cantaba la rana	**Translation:**
Cucú, cucú, debajo del aqua)	Cuckoo, cuckoo, sang the frog
	Cuckoo, cuckoo, underneath the water
Cucú, cucú, pasó un caballero	Cuckoo, cuckoo, a gentleman passed by
Cucú, cucú, con capa y sombrero	Cuckoo, cuckoo, with a cape and hat
Cucú, cucú, pasó una señora	Cuckoo, cuckoo, a woman passed by
Cucú, cucú, con traje de cola	Cuckoo, cuckoo, with a tailcoat
Cucú, cucú, pasó un marinero	Cuckoo, cuckoo, a sailor passed by
Cucú, cucú, vendiendo romero	Cuckoo, cuckoo, selling rosemary
Cucú, cucú, le pidió un ramito	Cuckoo, cuckoo, she asked for a branch
Cucú, cucú, no le quiso dar	Cuckoo, cuckoo, he did not want to give
Cucú, cucú, y se echó a llorar	Cuckoo, cuckoo, and she started to cry

Source: Ingrid Riquiac (Panajachel, Guatemala)

This song was composed by Luis Belmonte Bermúdez (1598–1650), a playwright from Spain, and was originally written in Old Spanish (or Old Castilian). Its original name was "Una rana hace ciento" (A Frog Makes a Hundred). It has undergone many different variations over time.

La Música (The Music)

De colores

The Colors

Translation:
Colorful, colorful are the fields in the springtime.
Colorful, colorful are the little birds that come from outside.
Colorful, colorful is the rainbow that we see shining,
and that is why great loves of many colors are pleasing to me,
and that is why great loves of many colors are pleasing to me.

Source: Nora Blass Hernández (San Juan de la Concepción, Nicaragua)

Enjoyed throughout Hispanic regions and the United States, it is believed that "De Colores" came to the Americas from Spain in the 1500s. It was adopted as the unofficial anthem for the United Farm Workers Movement in the United States in the 1950s and 1960s under the leadership of César Chavéz. Nora sang this with her students and would ask them what colors they see in the countryside.

Debajo de un botón

Under a Button

Translation:
Under a button that Martin found,
there was a mouse that was very little.
Very little was the mouse,
that Martin found under the button.

Directions: While singing *tin, tin, tin* and *ton, ton, ton*, clap once for each syllable. Change this action with each repetition of the song, for example, stomp feet, pat head, pat legs, etc.

Source: Emma Leticia Chávez and children at Escuela Modelo Inclusiva de Educación (Panajachel, Guatemala)

Leticia sang this with her first-grade class and led them through a variety of actions. This song is taught in schools to practice vocalizations.

Doña Cigüeña

Doña Cigüeña

Do - ña Ci - güe - ña pi - co co - lo - ra - do,
u - na pa - ti - ta se ha que - bra - do,
por e - so ca - mi - na con mu - cho cui - da - do,
con un pie en el sue - lo el o - tro le - van - ta - do.

Directions: The children sing while engaging in the following actions:
mm. 1–4: Open and close *beak* (two hands at mouth)
mm. 5–12: Rub one leg as if in pain
mm. 13–16: Hop on one foot
Repeat song while hopping on one foot.

Translation:
Mrs. Red-Beaked Stork,
her little leg has broken,
that's why she walks very carefully,
with one foot on the ground and the other raised.

Source: Damaris Santizo and children at Escuela Modelo Inclusiva de Educación (Panajachel, Guatemala)

Damaris joyfully led her young students in this active song as they tried to maintain their balance jumping on one foot while singing.

El árbol de la montaña

The Mountain Tree

El ár - bol de la mon - ta - ña, a - li - a - lo.

El ár - bol de la mon - ta - ña, a - li - a - lo.

E - se ár - bol tie - ne u - na ra - ma
E - sa ra - ma tie - ne u - na ho - ja
E - sa ho - ja tie - ne un ni - do
E - se ni - do tie - ne un hue - vo
E - se hue - vo tie - ne un pája - ro

ay, ay, ay, que be - lla ra - ma
                be - lla ho - ja
                be - llo ni - do
                gran____ hue - vo
                be - llo pája - ro

la ra - ma en el ár - bol____
la ho - ja en la ra - ma, la
el ni - do en la ho - ja, la
el hue - vo en el ni - do, el
el pája - ro en el hue - vo, el

a - li - a - lo.

La Música (The Music)

Singing Directions:
For first repeat:
> *m.5:* Sing first verse, then second verse
> *m. 7:* Sing second verse, then first verse

For second repeat:
> *m.5:* Sing first verse, then second, then third
> *m. 7:* Sing third verse, then second, first third

Continue this model for all verses.

Translation: (last verse)
The mountain tree, ah-li-ah-lo.
The mountain tree, ah-li-ah-lo.
That tree has a branch
That branch has a leaf
That leaf has a nest
That nest has an egg
That egg has a bird
Ay, ay, ay, what a beautiful bird.

The bird in the egg
the egg in the nest
the nest on the leaf
the leaf on the branch
the branch on the tree
ah-li-ah-lo.

Source: Isabel Águirre (Masaya, Nicaragua)

Isabel sang this beautiful song on the school playground. While melodically and rhythmically different, this additive song is lyrically similar to "The Green Grass Grew All Around" from the United States and "The Rattlin' Bog" from Ireland.

Canciones (Songs)

El gallo pinto

The Painted Rooster

Translation:
The rooster fell asleep
and this morning he did not sing.
Everyone awaits his cock-a-doodle-doo,
the sun did not rise because they did not hear him yet.

Source: La Familia Ical (Panajachel, Guatemala)

This is a Spanish language variant of the lullaby and round, "Le coq est mort" (The Rooster Is Dead) from France and "Let's Put the Rooster in the Stew" from England.

La Música (The Music)

El gatito

The Kitten

Ga - ti - to, ga - ti - to, di - ce tu ma - má,
que ya la co - mi - da en la mesa es - tá.
Pues, di - le a ma - mi - ta que no co - me - ré
por - que hay u - na fies - ta y a bai - lar ir - é.

Translation:
Kitty, kitty says your mom,
the food is already on the table.
Well, tell Mommy that I will not eat
because there is a party and I will dance.

Source: María Carmelina Ajcalón (Panajachel, Guatemala)

En el lejano bosque ▶

In the Faraway Forest

Singing Directions: Sing in unison or two-part round. Group two begins when group one is at the end of measure eight (*).

Translation:
In the distant forest the cuckoo sang.
Sitting in the foliage the owl answered.
Cuckoo he sang, cuckoo he sang, cuckoo, koo, koo, koo, koo.
Cuckoo he sang, cuckoo he sang, cuckoo, koo, koo, koo, koo.

Source: Isabel Águirre and children at La Amistad Escuela (Masaya, Nicaragua)

This is a Spanish language variant of "One Bright and Sunny Morning," a German round.

La Música (The Music)

Estrellita

Little Star

Es - tre - lli - ta, ¿dón-de_es - tás? Me pre - gun - to quién se - rás.

En el cie - lo_o en el mar, un dia - man - te de ver - dad.

Es - tre - lli - ta ¿dón-de_es - tás? Me pre - gun - to quién se - rás.

Translation:
Little star, where are you? I wonder who you are.
In the sky or in the sea, a true diamond.
Little star, where are you? I wonder who you are.

Source: Sarahí (Granada, Nicaragua)

A Spanish language variant of "Twinkle, Twinkle, Little Star," Sarahí would sing this with her young daughter.

Familia Dedo

Finger Family

Pa - pá de - do, pa - pá de - do, ¿dón - de es - tás?
A - quí es - toy, a - quí es - toy, ¿có - mo es - tás?

Directions: Hold hand up and tap the corresponding finger on the lyrics "*Aquí estoy, aquí estoy*" (m. 3). Repeat the song and substitute *papa dedo* with the next family member.

Papá dedo (thumb)
Mamá dedo (finger 1)
Hermana dedo (finger 2)
Hermano dedo (finger 3)
Bebé dedo (finger 4)

Students may choose different family structures.

Translation:
Father finger, father finger, where are you?
Here I am, here I am, how are you?
Mother finger . . .
Sister finger . . .
Brother finger . . .
Baby finger . . .

Source: Asalia Mercado (San Juan de la Concepción, Nicaragua)

Asalia provides dynamic instructions on how to engage with this song. She also suggests that children sing the song faster with each full repetition for language fluency.

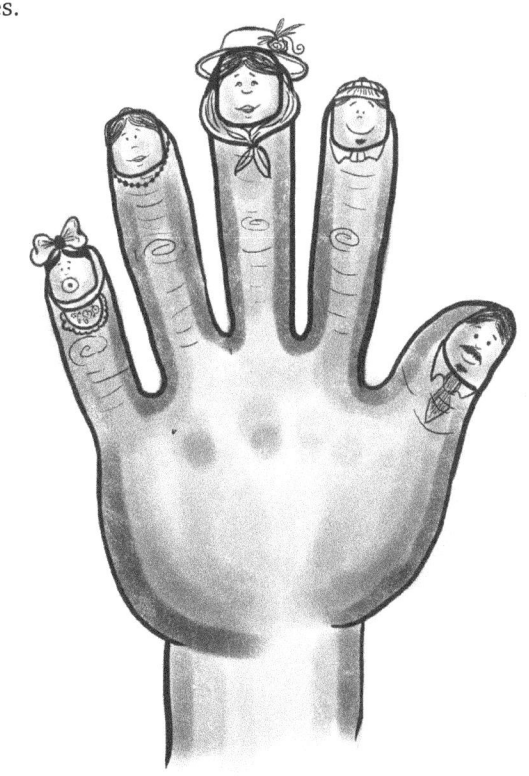

La Música (The Music)

Había un sapo

There Was a Toad

Directions:

mm. 1–2: Hands on hips, bend at knees on the steady beat

mm. 3–4: Move arms as if swimming

mm. 5–6: Pulse hands gently on chest

mm. 7–8: Wrap arms around self as if cold

mm. 9–10: Make circles with hands around eyes

mm. 11–12: Place hands on sides of mouth

mm. 13–14: Point to sky

m. 15: Jump up while pointing to sky

Translation:

There was a toad, toad, toad, that swam in the river, river, river
with his green, green, green suit, he was dying of cold, cold, cold.
Mrs. Frog, Frog, Frog sang, sang, sang to me
that I had a friend, friend, friend named Jesus.

Sources: Teacher and children at Escuela Modelo Inclusiva de Educación (Panajachel, Guatemala), Dariela and children at La Mariposa Preschool (San Juan de la Concepción, Nicaragua), Children at Escuela Pablo Antonio Cuadra (Granada, Nicaragua)

Hazlo conmigo

Do It With Me

Directions: The children sing while engaging in the following actions:
mm. 1–4: A leader creates a movement for the others to copy (for example, clapping)
m. 5: The leader changes the location of this movement to one place and then another (for example, clapping up high and then down low)
m. 6: The leader slows the movement down and then speeds it up
mm. 7–10: The leader performs the same movement as in measures 1–4
The song is repeated with a different movement.

Translation:
Do it with me, follow, follow me. Do it with me follow, follow me.
Do it like this, do it there, slowly or quickly.
Do it with me, follow, follow me. Do it with me follow, follow me.

Source: Jocelyn, a fourth-grade student at Escuela Pablo Antonio Cuadra (Granada, Nicaragua)

On the school playground during recess, Jocelyn gave a joyous demonstration of this song with accompanying movements. One lyrical variant for measure 5 is "Hazlo acá, hazlo allá" (Do it here, do it there).

La Música (The Music)

La hormiguita

The Little Ant

Es - ta - ba una hor - mi - gui - ta sen - tada en un bal - cón

con su ves - tida de se - da, za - pa - tos de cha - rol.

Bai - la - ba, can - ta - ba, es - ta - ba muy con - ten - ta se pu - so a bai - lar

y dió la me - dia vuel - ta al suelo fue a pa - rar.

Directions: The children sing while engaging in the following actions:
mm. 5–7: Dance in place
m. 8: Turn around once
m. 9: Sit down

Translation:
There was an ant sitting on a balcony
with her silk dress, patent leather shoes.
They danced, they sang, they were very happy they started to dance
and turned around and fell to the ground.

Source: Nora Blass Hernández (San Juan de la Concepción, Nicaragua)

Nora gave an active demonstration of this song on the patio of her house. Her daughter, Lidia, joined her singing on the last phrase.

La lechuza

The Owl

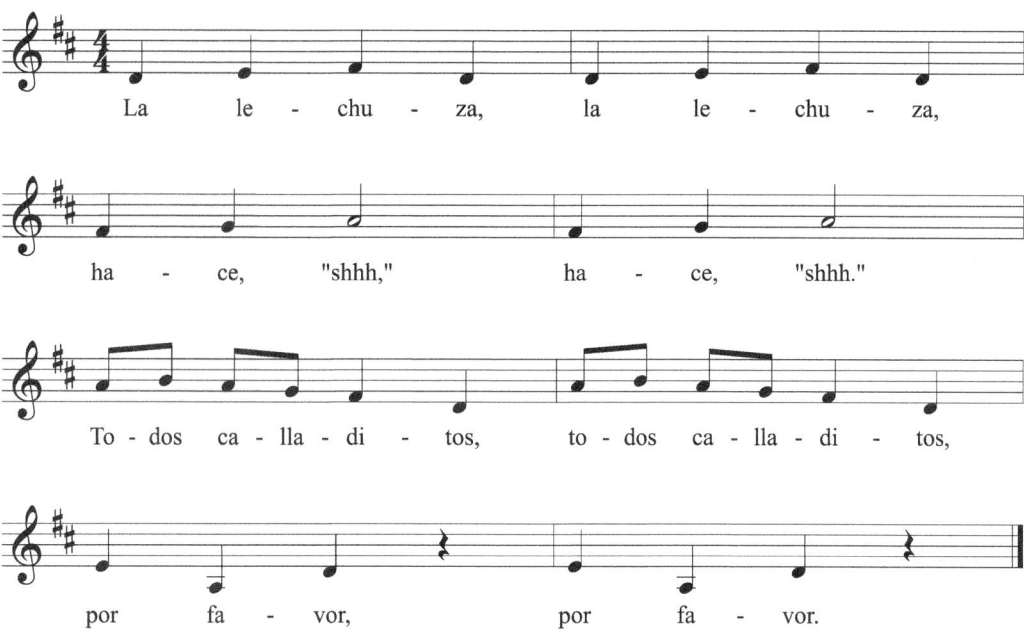

Translation:
The owl, the owl,
goes "shhh," goes "shhh."
Everyone quiet, everyone quiet,
please, please.

Sources: Isabel Águirre and children at La Amistad Escuela (Masaya, Nicaragua), Nora Blass Hernández (San Juan de la Concepción, Nicaragua)

Set to the melody of "Frère Jacques," this variant is used in schools to encourage quiet in classrooms. Isabel dynamically describes a scene of an owl in nature before singing the song with the children.

La Música (The Music)

La mané

The Hand

Que lo baile, que lo baile, que lo baile, que lo baile,
que lo baile, que lo baile, que lo bailará muy bien!
La mané se irá poniendo donde vaya diciendo
donde vaya diciendo, la mané se va a poner.
Que lo baile, que lo baile, que lo baile todo el mundo
y el que no sepa bailar una prenda pagará.

Chant: ¡Una mané! (hold out hand)
¡En la cabecé! (place hand on head)
¡Y la otra mané! (hold out other hand)
¡En el hombro! (place that hand shoulder)

Directions:
Song: The children sing while dancing freely.
Chant: The leader calls out each command with an accompanying action and the group responds after with the same command and action (call–response):
The song is repeated while keeping hands on those body parts.
The leader improvises new commands and actions for each repetition.

Translation:
Let them dance, let them dance
Let them dance, they will dance it very well.
The hand will go where I am saying,
where I am saying, the hand will go.
Let them dance, let them dance, let everyone dance
and whoever does not know how to dance a punishment you will pay.

One hand!
On the head!
And the other hand!
On the shoulder!

Sources: Nicolasa Peréz (Panajachel, Guatemala), Teacher and children at Escuela Modelo Inclusiva de Educación, (Panajachel, Guatemala)

La Música (The Music)

La pequeña araña

The Little Spider

U - na pe - que - ña a - ra - ña su - bió a la ca - na - le - ta.

Vi - no la llu - via y se la lle - vó.

Sa - lió el sol y se se - có la llu - via

y la pe - que - ña a - ra - ña o - tra vez su - bió.

Translation:
A little spider climbed up the waterspout.
The rain came and washed him out.
Out came the sun and dried up the rain and
the little spider climbed up another time.

Sources: Isabel Águirre and children at Escuela La Amistad (Masaya, Nicaragua),

María Carmelina Ajcalón (Panajachel, Guatemala)

A Spanish language variant of "The Itsy Bitsy Spider," Isabel prefaces the song by asking the children about the spider, the waterspout, and the sun as they collectively describe the events in this song.

La rana

The Frog

Es-ta-ba *la ra-na* can-tan-do de-ba-jo del a - gua.

Cuan-do la ra-na se pu-so a can-tar, vi-no *el sa-po* y lo hi-zo ca-llar.

Estaba *la rana, el sapo,* cantando debajo del agua.
Cuando *el sapo* se puso a cantar vino *el gato* y lo hizo callar.

Estaba *la rana, el sapo, el gato* cantando debajo del agua.
Cuando *el gato* se puso a cantar vino *el perro* y lo hizo callar.

Estaba *la rana, el sapo, el gato, el perro* cantando debajo del agua.
Cuando *el perro* se puso a cantar vino *la vaca* y lo hizo callar.

Estaba *la rana, el sapo, el gato, el perro, la vaca* cantando debajo del agua.
Cuando *la vaca* se puso a cantar vino *el burro* y lo hizo callar.

Estaba *la rana, el sapo, el gato, el perro, la vaca, el burro* cantando debajo del agua.
Cuando *el burro* se puso a cantar vino *el mono* y lo hizo callar.

Estaba *la rana, el sapo, el gato, el perro, la vaca, el burro, el mono* cantando debajo del agua.
Cuando *el mono* se puso a cantar vino *mis amigos* y lo hizo callar.

Singing Directions:
An additive song, sing each verse with the same melody, continuing the same rhythm and pitch (F, *do*) for the *list of animals*.

Translation: (last verse)
The frog, the toad, the cat, the dog, the cow, the donkey, the monkey were singing under the water. When the monkey started to sing, my friends came and made them be quiet.

Informants: Merlyn Rubí Celada García and children at Escuela Modelo Inclusiva de Educación (Panajachel, Guatemala)

La Música (The Music)

La vaca lechera

The Dairy Cow

(Tengo una vaca lechera.
No es una vaca cualquiera.
Me da leche condensada
para toda la semana,
tolón, tolón, tolón, tolón.)

Un cencerro le he comprado
a mi vaca le ha gustado.
Se pasea por el prado,
mata moscas con el rabo,
tolón, tolón, tolón, tolón

Translation:
I have a dairy cow.
She is not just any cow.
She gives me condensed milk
for the whole week,
clang, clang, clang, clang.

I have bought a cowbell
and my cow liked it.
She walks through the meadow,
she kills flies with her tail,
clang, clang, clang, clang.

Source: María Carmelina Ajcalón (Panajachel, Guatemala)

Composed by Fernando García Morcillo in the mid-1900s in Spain, it is believed that his inspiration was drawn from a train trip from Madrid to Galicia where, from his window, he saw many cows grazing in the field. The song uses onomatopoeia, as "*tolón, tolón*" is an imitation of ringing cow bells.

Canciones (Songs)

La vaca Lola

Lola the Cow

La vaca Lola, la vaca Lola
tiene cabeza y tiene cola.
La vaca Lola, la vaca Lola
tiene cabeza y tiene cola y hace, "¡mu!"

Translation:
Lola the cow, Lola the cow
has a head and a tail.
Lola the cow, Lola the cow
has a head and a tail and goes, "moo!"

Source: Isabel Águirre and children at Escuela La Amistad (Masaya, Nicaragua)

Isabel and the children engage in responsive movements to the lyrics while singing this playful song.

La Música (The Music)

La vaquita

The Little Cow

Yo ten-go u-na va-qui-ta que ha-ce, "mu mu, mu,"
y un chi-vi-to blan-co que ha-ce, "meh meh, meh."
Y to-das las ma-ña-nas los lle-vo al co-rral.
Me dan muy bue-na le-che que me a-li-men-ta-rá.

Translation:
I have a little cow that goes, "moo, moo, moo,"
and a little white goat that goes, "meh, meh, meh."
And every morning I take them to the farmyard.
They give me very good milk that will feed me.

Source: Nora Blass Hernández (San Juan de la Concepción, Nicaragua)

Nora sang this with her students to practice the consonant *m* and the vowel sounds *oo* and *eh*.

Las calaveras

The Skeletons

Cuan - do el re - loj   mar - ca la u - na   las ca - la - ve - ras   sa - len de sus tum - bas.

Tum - ba - la - ca, tum - ba - la - ca, tum - ba - la,   tum - ba - la - ca, tum - ba - la - ca, tum - ba - la.

Cuando el reloj marca	When the clock shows
la UNA las calaveras salen de sus tumbas	ONE the skeletons come out of their graves
las DOS las calaveras comen arroz	TWO the skeletons eat rice
las TRES las calaveras se bailan al revés	THREE the skeletons dance backwards
las CUATRO las calaveras se van al teatro	FOUR the skeletons go to the theater
las CINCO las calaveras se pagan un brinco	FIVE the skeletons jump
las SEIS las calaveras juegan ajedrez	SIX the skeletons play chess
las SIETE las calaveras comen un filete	SEVEN the skeletons eat steak
las OCHO las calaveras comen un bizcocho	EIGHT the skeletons eat cake
las NUEVE las calaveras juegan en la nieve	NINE the skeletons play in the snow
las DIEZ las calaveras se pisan los pies	TEN the skeletons step on their feet
las ONCE las calaveras pintan el bronce	ELEVEN the skeletons paint bronze
las DOCE las calaveras se desconocen	TWELVE the skeletons are unknown
la UNA las calaveras regresan a sus tumbas	ONE the skeletons return to their grave

Directions: The children sing while engaging in the following actions:

mm. 1–4: Create movements for each verse

mm. 5–6: Turn forearms around each other on right side of body

mm. 7–8: Turn forearms around each other on left side of body

La Música (The Music)

Source: Damaris Santizo and children at Escuela Modelo Inclusiva de Educación (Panajachel, Guatemala)

The variant "Los esqueletos" (Spain) was sung in the 1900s as a street processional. The singers carried figurines made with pumpkins with carved-out faces placed on poles.

Las manitos ▶

The Little Hands

Con mis manitos yo escribo, yo escribo.
Con mis manitos escribo yo.

Con mis manitos me peino, me peino.
Con mis manitos me peino yo.

Con mis manitos me baño, me baño.
Con mis manitos me baño yo.

Directions: The children create movements for each verse.

Translation:
With my little hands I eat, I eat.
With my little hands I eat.

With my little hands I write, I write . . .

With my little hands I brush my hair, I brush my hair . . .

With my little hands I take a bath, I take a bath . . .

Source: Nora Blass Hernández (San Juan de la Concepción, Nicaragua)

Nora and her students would sing about many things they could do with their hands, allowing for responsive movement and lyrical improvisation.

La Música (The Music)

Las verduras

The Vegetables

En el cam-po ver-de__ hay mu-chas ver-dur-as.__
U-nas son muy sua-ves y o-tras son muy du-ras.
Las co-me_el co-ne-jo,__ las pi-ca_el gu-sa-no,
a to-dos no-so-tros nos man-tie-nen sa-no.

Translation:
In the green field there are many vegetables.
Some are very soft and others are very hard.
The rabbit eats them, the worm bites them,
and they keep us all healthy.

Source: Nora Blass Hernández (San Juan de la Concepción, Nicaragua)

Nora sang this with her students and included discussions about the variety of vegetables grown in Nicaragua, how they were harvested, and their important nutrition.

Los pajaritos ▶

The Little Birds

Los pa - ja - ri - tos que van por el ai - re,

vue - lan, vue - lan, vue - lan, vue - lan, vue - lan.

Los pececitos que van por el agua,
nadan, nadan, nadan, nadan, nadan.

Los conejitos que van por la hierba,
saltan, saltan, saltan, saltan, saltan.

Los caballitos que van por el campo,
trotan, trotan, trotan, trotan, trotan.

Directions: The children create movements for each verse: flying, swimming, jumping, and trotting. The teacher or children can create new verses with different animals and movements.

The little birds that fly through the air,
they fly, they fly, they fly, they fly, they fly.

The little fish that go through the water,
they swim . . .

The little rabbits that go through the grass,
they jump . . .

The little horses that go through the field,
they trot . . .

Sources: Teacher and children at Escuela República de Cuba (San Juan de la Concepción, Nicaragua)

This sweet song has possibilities for lyric and movement improvisation as children and teachers add different animals, locations, and actions.

La Música (The Music)

Los patitos

The Ducklings

Translation:

The ducklings go to the water wanting to swim.
The duck goes ahead of the ducklings in back.
In the cool lake the ducklings swim,
moving their wings to move like little boats.
They dunk their heads, they move their tails,
and the youngest calls out to mama.

Formation 1: Standing circle with leader as part of circle

Directions 1:
mm. 1–4: Clap to the steady beat
mm. 5–6: Walk forward on the steady beat
mm. 7–8: Walk backward on the steady beat
mm. 9–16: Flap *wings*
mm. 17–18: Lean head toward center of circle
mm. 19–20: Wag *tail*
mm. 21–24: Flap *wings*

Formation 2: The children form a single line behind a leader (mother duck)

Directions 2: The children sing while the mother duck leads the children freely around the space.

Source: Isabel Águirre and children at La Amistad Escuela (Masaya, Nicaragua)

La Música (The Music)

Los pollitos

The Little Chicks

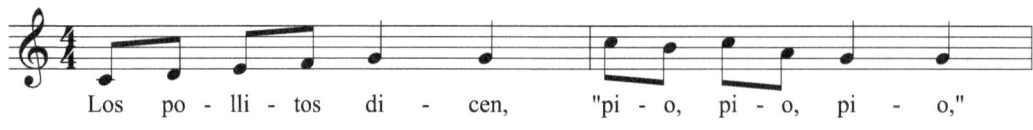
Los po-lli-tos di-cen, "pi-o, pi-o, pi-o,"

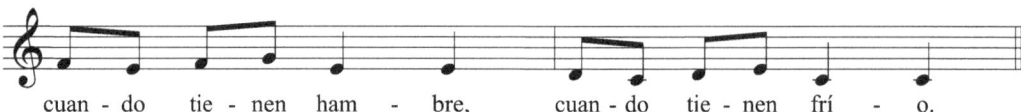
cuan-do tie-nen ham-bre, cuan-do tie-nen frí-o.

La gallina busca el maíz y el trigo,
les da la comida y les presta abrigo

Bajo sus dos alas acurrucaditos,
duermen los pollitos hasta el otro día.

Translation:
The little chicks say, "peep, peep, peep,"
when they are hungry, when they are cold.

The hen is looking for corn and wheat,
she gives them food and lends them shelter.

Under her two wings huddling,
the little chicks sleep until another day.

Source: Nicolasa Peréz (Panajachel, Guatemala)

A nursery rhyme and lullaby from Spain, this song is well known throughout many Hispanic regions.

Marinero ▶

Sailor

Ma - ri - ne - ro que se fue a la mar y mar y mar,

pa - ra ver que po - dí - a ver y ver y ver.

Y lo ú - ni - co que pu - do ver y ver y ver,

fue el fon - do de la mar y mar y mar.

Translation:
The sailor who went to the sea and sea and sea,
to see what they could see and see and see.
And the only thing they could see and see and see,
was the bottom of the sea and sea and sea.

Source: Dariela and children at La Mariposa Preschool (San Juan de la Concepción, Nicaragua)

La Música (The Music)

Mi burro

My Donkey

A mi burro, mi burro le due-le la ca-be-za,
le due-len las o-re-jas,
le due-le la gar-gan-ta,
le due-le_el co-ra-zón,
le due-len las ro-di-llas,
le due-len las pe-zu-ñas,
ya no le due-le na-da,

el me-di-co le man-da u-na go-rri-ta grue-sa,
que las pon-ga muy tie-sa,
u-na bu-fan-da blan-ca,
go-ti-tas de li-món,
un pla-to de na-ti-lla,
que se-ca de las u-ñas,
un ju-go de na-ran-ja,

u - na go - rri - ta grue - sa
que las pon - ga muy tie - sa
u - na bu - fan - da blan - ca
go - ti - tas de li - món
un pla - to de na - ti - lla
que se - ca de las u - ñas
un ju - go de na - ran - ja

Mi burro en-fermo es-tá. Mi burro en-fermo es-tá.

Canciones (Songs)

Directions: An additive song. With each repeat in line three, start on the subsequent lyric line then sing all the phrases above. The children can create actions to accompany the lyrics.

My donkey, my donkey,	his head hurts	the doctor ordered	a thick hat
	his ears hurt		put it on tight
	his throat hurts		a white scarf
	his heart hurts		lemon drops
	his knees hurt		a plate of custard
	his hooves hurt		to cut your nails
	nothing hurts anymore		orange juice

My donkey is sick. My donkey is sick.

Source: Three children at Escuela La Amistad (Masaya, Nicaragua)

Three young boys tenderly sang this favorite song of theirs with accompanying actions on the playground during recess.

La Música (The Music)

Panadero

Baker

Translation:
Baker, baker,
makes bread, makes bread.
Give it to me hot, give it to me hot.
Ding, dong, dang. Ding, dong, dang.

Source: Sarahí (Granada, Nicaragua)

Set to the melody of "Frère Jacques," Sarahí would sing this song with her young daughter.

Periquito

Parakeet

Directions:

mm. 5, 13: Point up *mm. 7, 15:* Point in front
mm. 6, 14: Point down *mm. 8, 16:* Point in back

This song has additive actions. At the end of the song, the leader calls out an action, for example, "*pulgares afueras*" (thumbs out), and the song is repeated while holding thumbs out front. The leader chooses another action, for example, "*codos a centro*" (elbows in), and the children repeat the song with thumbs out and elbows touching each other. Continue adding different commands, such as "*un ojo cerrado*" (one eye closed) or "*una lengua afuera*" (tongue out).

Translation:
The parakeet, the parakeet, looks like their *mom*,
above, below, ahead, behind. (repeat with *dad*)

Source: María Carmelina Ajcalón (Panajachel, Guatemala)

Carmelina remembered learning this song in elementary school. She now sings it with children and sometimes substitutes different animals for *mamá* and *papá*.

La Música (The Music)

Pin Pon

Pin Pon

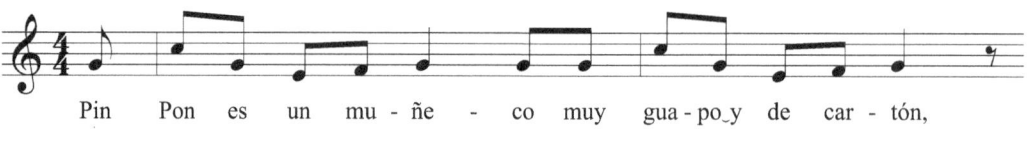

Pin Pon es un muñe-co muy gua-po y de car-tón,

se la-va la ca-ri-ta con a-gua y con ja-bón.

Se peina los cabellos, se cambia el pantalón,
se va para la escuela y aprende su lección.

Pin Pon dame la mano con un fuerte apretón,
yo quiero ser tu amigo, Pin Pon, Pin Pon, Pin Pon.

Translation:
Pin Pon is a doll, very handsome and made of cardboard,
they wash their little face with water and soap.

They comb their hair, they change their pants,
they leave for school to learn.

Pin Pon give me your hand with a strong squeeze,
I want to be your friend, Pin Pon, Pin Pon, Pin Pon.

Sources: Damaris Santizo and children at Escuela Modelo Inclusiva de Educación (Panajachel, Guatemala), María Carmelina Ajcalón and Nicolasa Peréz (Panajachel, Guatemala)

A very well-known song throughout Guatemala, this is a simpler variant of a song written for the television show and lead character *Pin Pon*, a popular Chilean children's program in the early 1970s. A melodic variant from Carmelina and Nicolasa can be found on the companion website.

Salió la gallina ▶

The Chicken Came Out

Translation:
The hen went out, went out for a walk with her three chicks by the barn.
Doña Cocorico makes her see that she must have all of her chickens.
Listen chicken, you can lose the little chickens, they will be eaten by
the rogue fox or the hawk.

Source: Nora Blass Hernández (San Juan de la Concepción, Nicaragua)

La Música (The Music)

Salta, mi conejito

Jump, My Bunny

Sal - ta, mi co - ne - ji - to, co - me su za - ca - ti - to,

pa - ra tus o - re - ji - tas mi co - ne - ji - to, co - ne - jo mí - o.

Tri - ste es - tán los cam - pos des - de que tú te fui - ste

pe - ro yo es-toy a - le - gre por-que te can - to mi co - ne - ji - to, co - ne - jo mí - o.

Translation:
Jump, my bunny, eat your little grassy plant,
for your little ears my bunny, rabbit of mine.
The fields are sad since you left
but I'm happy because I sing to my bunny of mine.

Source: Teacher at La Mariposa Spanish School (San Juan de la Concepción, Nicaragua)

Sol, solecito ▶

Little Sun

Sol, sol-e-ci-to ca-lién-ta me un po-qui-to,
Lu-na, lu-ne-ra,___ cas - ca be - le - ra,

por hoy por ma-ña-na por to-da la se-ma-na.
___ cin - co po-lli-tos y u - na ter-ner-a.

Ca - ra - col, ca - ra - col, a la u - na sa - le el sol,

sa-le Pi-no-cho to-can-do el tam - bor con u - na cu-cha-ra y un te-ne-dor.

Translation:
Little sun, warm me a little for today,
for tomorrow and for the whole week.
Moon, moon, whimsical moon,
five chicks and a calf.
Snail, snail, at one o'clock the sun rises,
Pinocchio comes out playing the drum with a spoon and a fork.

Sources: Isabel Águirre and children at Escuela La Amistad (Masaya, Nicaragua), children at Escuela República de Cuba (San Juan de la Concepción, Nicaragua)

Historically, this Spanish song from the 1700s accompanied a ritual directed at the moon to invoke good fortune and riches.

La Música (The Music)

Soy una taza

I Am a Cup

Ta-za, te-te-ra, cu-cha-ra, cu-cha-rón,

pla-to hon-do, pla-to pla-no, cu-chi-lli-to, te-ne-dor,

sa-le-ro, a-zu-ca-re-ro, ba-ti-do-ra, olla ex-prés. ¡Chú, chú!

Soy u-na ta-za, u-na te-te-ra, u-na cu-cha-ra, un cu-cha-rón,

un pla-to hon-do, un pla-to pla-no, un cu-chi-lli-to, un te-ne-dor.

Soy un sa-le-ro, a-zu-ca-re-ro, la ba-ti-do-ra, o-lla ex-prés. ¡Chú, chu!

Ta-za, te-te-ra, cu-cha-ra, cu-cha-rón, pla-to hon-do, pla-to pla-no, cu-chi-lli-to, te-ne-dor,

sa-le-ro a-zu-ca-re-ro, ba-ti-do-ra, olla ex-prés. ¡Chú, chú!

Canciones (Songs)

Translation and Directions: Children engage in these actions for each word:

| taza (cup) | tetera (teapot) | cuchara (spoon) | cucharón (ladle) |

| plato llano (deep dish plate) | plato plano (flat plate) | cuchillito (little knife) | tenedor (fork) |

| salero (salt shaker) | azucarero (sugar bowl) | batidora (blender) | olla exprés (pressure cooker) |

I am a cup, a teapot, a spoon, a ladle,
a deep dish plate, a flat plate, a little knife, a fork.
I am a salt shaker, sugar bowl, the blender, pressure cooker. Choo, choo!

Sources: Teachers at La Mariposa Spanish School (San Juan de la Concepción, Nicaragua), Dariela and children at La Mariposa Preschool (San Juan de la Concepción, Nicaragua)

This traditional song was extremely popular with children, families, and schools in Nicaragua. Frequently, children and adults engaged in the song and actions accompanied by a recording by *CantaJuego*, recording artists from Spain.

La Música (The Music)

Tengo una casita

I Have a Little House

Directions:

mm. 1–4: Outline the shape of a house with fingers

mm. 5–8: Mimic the rising of smoke with one hand

mm. 9–16: Pretend to knock on a door

With each repetition the outlined house gets larger (*mm. 1–4*) and the knocking is more exaggerated (*mm. 9–16*).

Translation:

I have a little house that is like this, like this,
through the chimney the smoke comes out like this, like this,
that when I go to enter I knock like this, like this, like this,
that when I go to enter I knock like this, like this, like this.

Source: Children at Escuela Pablo Antonio Cuadra (Granada, Nicaragua)

Un amigo ▶

A Friend

Un a-mi-go me en-se-ño a can-tar es-ta can-ción.
Un a-mi-go me en-señ-ó a can-tar a-sí.

Formation: Sitting circle with each child or small group assigned to a different animal

Directions: After each repetition of the song, one child or small group makes their animal sounds.

Translation:
A friend taught me to sing this song.
A friend taught me to sing like this.

Source: María Carmelina Ajcalón (Panajachel, Guatemala)

Carmelina sings this song with children to teach animal names and encourage vocal exploration.

La Música (The Music)

Un elefante (Guatemala)

An Elephant

Dos elefantes se columpiaban con una tela de una araña.
Y como vieron que resistia fueron a llamar a otro elefante.

Repeat the song as many times as desired, increasing the number of elephants.

Translation:
An elephant was swinging
on a spider web.
And as they saw the web could withstand it
they went to call another elephant.

Sources: Damaris Santizo and children at Escuela Modelo Inclusiva de Educación (Panajachel, Guatemala), María Carmelina Ajcalón (Panajachel, Guatemala)

This is a popular children's song among many Hispanic countries. Melodic variants observed in both Guatemala and Nicaragua are included in this collection.

Un elefante (Nicaragua)

An Elephant

Un elefante se balanceaba
sobre la tela de una araña.
Como veía que resistía
fueron a llamar otro elefante.

Dos elefantes se balanceaban sobre la tela de una araña.
Como vieron que resistía fueron a llamar a otro elefante.

Repeat the song as many times as desired, increasing the number of elephants.

Translation:
An elephant was rocking
on a spider web.
As they saw the web could withstand it
they went to call another elephant.

Sources: Teachers at La Mariposa Spanish School (San Juan de la Concepción, Nicaragua), children at Escuela República de Cuba (San Juan de la Concepción, Nicaragua)

La Música (The Music)

Vamos a remar

Let's Row

Va - mos a re - mar en u - na lan - chi - ta,
rá - pi - do, rá - pi - do, rá - pi - do, rá - pi - do, en u - na lan - chi - ta.

Translation:
Let's row in a small boat,
quickly, quickly, quickly, quickly, in a little boat.

Source: La Familia González (Panajachel, Guatemala)

This is a variant if "Row, Row, Row Your Boat" and can be sung in a round.

Yo me gozo

I Rejoice

Translation:
I rejoice Monday, I rejoice Tuesday, I rejoice Wednesday.
I rejoice Thursday, I rejoice Friday, Saturday, too.
Sunday arrives, I continue rejoicing and do you know why?
Because I have Christ, he gives me life, I rejoice in him.
Because I have Christ, he gives me life, I rejoice in him.

Sources: Asalia Mercado (San Juan de la Concepción, Nicaragua), Isabel Águirre and children at Escuela La Amistad (Masaya, Nicaragua)

Christianity is a prominent religion in Nicaragua and religious songs are enjoyed in families and schools to foster and communicate these beliefs.

La Música (The Music)

Jun Ti Sanik

The Ant

Jun ti sa - nik nu sa - maj pa sa - na - yí
xi taq sa - nik ye sa - maj pa sa - na - yí

taq xa - pon Jun chik ja - ru - pe ri xki - b'an. Ka' - i, ka'
taq xa - pon jun chik ja - ru - pe ri xki - b'an. O - xi, o

Jun ti sanik nu samaj pa sanayí
Taq xapon jun chik jampe ri xkib'an'

Oxi, oxi taq sanik ye samaj pa sanayi
Taq xapon jun chik jampe ri xkib'an'

Kaji, kaji taq sanik ye samaj pa sanayi
Taq xapon jun chik jampe ri xkib'an'

Wo'o, wo'o taq sanik ye samaj pa sanayi
Taq xapon jun chik jampe ri xkib'an'

Waqi', waqi' taq sanik ye samaj pa sanayi
Taq xapon jun chik jampe ri xkib'an'

Wuqú, Wuqú taq sanik ye samaj pa sanayi
Taq xapon jun chik jampe ri xkib'an'

Waqxaqi', waqxaqi' taq sanik ye samaj pa sanayi
Taq xapon jun chik jampe ri xkib'an'

Translation:
An ant works in the anthill. When another arrived how many will there be?
Two, two ants work in the anthill. When another arrived how many will there be?
Three, three ants work in the anthill. When another arrived how many will there be?
Four, four . . .

Source: María Carmelina Ajcalón (Buena Vista, Guatemala)

This song communicates the importance of teamwork. Carmelina shared that working together in groups is very important and preferable in Mayan culture and adults and children sing this song to support this message. A pronunciation guide for this song in Kaqchikel is available on the companion website.

La Música (The Music)

Ni Tz'unun

The Hummingbird

Ni-ro-pop, ni-ro-pop la ri tz'u nún, ka nu-ju-lu-lej nu-pam la ti ket-z'ij,

ni-ro-pop, ni-ro-pop la ti tz'u nún, ka nu-ju-lu-lej nu-pam la ti ket-z'ij,

ni-be ke-la' ni-pe ke-re' ti-qa-cha-pa'— la ti tz'u-nun

ni-be ke-la' ni-pe ke-re' ti-qa-cha-pa'— la ti-tz'u-nun.

Translation:
Fly, fly the hummingbird is sucking the nectar from the flower (2xs)
Go there, come here or there, there are hummingbirds (2xs)

Source: María Carmelina Ajcalón (Buena Vista, Guatemala)

A song about hummingbirds, the words are meant to capture the beauty of nature and the animal world. There are many Mayan legends that include the hummingbird, one of which claims that their feathers have magical powers. A pronunciation guide for this song in Kaqchikel is available on the companion website.

Ri Utzil Iwach

Greetings

Sa-qar ta-ta, sa-qar na-na, utz i-wach, utz i-wach,

roj ri utz ma-tiox, roj ri utz ma-tiox, ma-tiox k'a-ri, ma-tiox k'a-ri.

Xbaq'ij tata, xbaq'ij nana
Utz iwach, utz iwach
Roj ri utz matiox, Roj ri utz matiox
Matiox k'ari, matiox k'ari

Xqaq'ij tata, xqaq'ij nana
Utz iwach, utz iwach
Roj ri utz matiox, Roj ri utz matiox
Matiox k'ari, matiox k'ari

Xokaq'a tata, xokaq'a nana
Utz iwach, utz iwach
Roj ri utz matiox, Roj ri utz matiox
Matiox k'ari, matiox k'ari

Translation:
Good morning, sir. Good morning, madam. How are you? How are you?
We are well, we are well. Oh, how great! Oh, how great!

Good morning, sir. Good late morning, madam. How are you? How are you?
We are well, we are well. Oh, how great! Oh, how great!

Good afternoon, sir. Good afternoon, madam. How are you? How are you?
We are well, we are well. Oh, how great! Oh, how great!

Good evening, sir. Good evening, madam. How are you? How are you?
We are well, we are well. Oh, how great! Oh, how great!

La Música (The Music)

Source: María Carmelina Ajcalón (Buena Vista, Guatemala)

Carmelina expressed that this song is shared to instill values and respect in young children when interacting with their elders. A pronunciation guide for this song in Kaqchikel is available on the companion website.

PART 3
Beyond the Songs

Culturally Responsive and Sustaining Pedagogies

Music teachers must think, engage, and teach beyond repertoire. We want children to feel safe, engaged, understood, nurtured, valued, and part of an environment that offers a meaningful and relevant education. Embedding the songs in this book in a framework of culturally responsive and sustaining pedagogies is very important. This chapter provides an overview of these strategies as inspiration for further study. While specific suggestions for teaching the songs are included at the front of the book, this section discusses broader ideas and issues.

The curriculum, pedagogical strategies, and school environment need to affirm and include students from all ethnicities and cultures. Discriminatory practices based on race, ethnicity, and language background often marginalize Black, Brown, and Indigenous children, and these inequities persist despite progress made since the Civil Rights Movement in the 1960s. Multicultural education, which emerged as a powerful reform movement, continues to challenge educators to decenter curriculum and pedagogical practices that privilege white Eurocentric ideologies. Gloria Ladson-Billings (1994, 1995), who introduced the pedagogical framework Culturally Relevant Pedagogy in the 1990s, argues that schools can successfully engage and empower learners who historically have been marginalized. The framework holds high expectations for student learning and intellectual growth and creates opportunities for students to build both cultural competence, which is the ability to remain grounded in one's culture of origin while being able to successfully navigate at least one other culture, and critical consciousness, which includes the ability to think critically about social, cultural, economic, and political problems in the world and skill in being change agents.

Building on the work of Ladson-Billings, Geneva Gay (2018) developed the framework of Culturally Responsive Teaching, which foregrounds "cultural knowledge, prior experiences, frames of references, and performance styles of ethnically diverse students to make learning encounters more relevant to and effective for them" (p. 36). With an emphasis on teaching practices, diverse resources and materials are integrated into all subject and skill areas and diversity in learning styles and culturally specific ways of knowing are valued and implemented in formal curricula. This approach aims to liberate students from oppressive educational practices and work toward school and societal transformation. Emphasis is placed on developing positive relationships with students and creating caring classroom communities. Teachers are called upon to challenge racial and cultural stereotypes and work toward social justice and academic equity.

Paris and Alim's more recent conceptualization of Cultural Sustaining Pedagogy lovingly challenges and extends the work of Ladson-Billings and Gay. Paris and Alim argue that culturally relevant and responsive pedagogies are too accepting of mainstream norms and require students, rather than schools, to make accommodations to align with deeply entrenched pedagogical, social, and cultural expectations that continue to reflect European middle-class values. This creates a cultural disconnect for students who enter formal schooling with set learning patterns and ways of knowing shaped by a home culture that differs from school culture. Paris and Alim (2017) assert that these students and families are being asked to "lose or deny their language, literacies, cultures, and histories in order to achieve in schools" (p. 1) and educational theorists report that these cultural incongruencies are failing Black, Brown, and Indigenous students. The goal of this pedagogy is to sustain students' languages, literacies, and cultural ways of being by shifting the norms historically deemed necessary for success. Kinloch (2017) states, "In this way students reject narratives of failure that demonize their intellectual acuity and cultural competences, and they accept narratives of belonging that locate them within the process and project of schooling" (p. 38). Lee and McCarty (2017) propose a pedagogical extension to the work of Paris and Alim called Culturally Sustaining/Revitalizing Pedagogies, which acts to revitalize that which has been disrupted by colonization. When European nations established colonies in the Americas, Indigenous cultures, religions, and languages were systematically destroyed, leaving lasting legacies in these countries. This pedagogical strategy strives to reclaim traditions and ways of being that have been ignored or erased from society.

All of these pedagogies challenge the deficit mindset, which views diverse languages and cultures as barriers to learning and the resulting disparities in success as "achievement gaps." Paris and Alim respond to this notion by posing the question, "Whose gap is it?" and demand that the cultures, experiences, and ways of knowing of Black, Brown, and Indigenous students of color, their families, and communities be centered in the classroom.

Many fields of education are reviewing processes through these pedagogical lenses to improve practices and outcomes and to foster a sense of belonging and success for all students. As the field of music education has seen an incredible growth of multicultural resources over the past several decades, it is imperative that we embed these materials into frameworks that are meaningful, authentic, and affirming. What could culturally responsive and sustaining teaching look like in the classroom? There is no "checklist" a teacher can use to become a culturally responsive and sustaining educator; rather, it requires learning, critical reflection, self-awareness, cultural humility, a commitment to getting to know students and families, and attention to one's craft. These pedagogies require a disposition for social justice and equity, and teachers must possess a desire to critically reflect on and challenge their own assumptions, biases, values, and norms. These are essential attributes of teachers who engage in culturally responsive and sustaining pedagogies. Aligning with these approaches, the sections that follow present a few broad strategies to consider along with the "Suggestions for Teachers" in Part 1 of this book. The inclusion of these recommendations serves as a point of entry, inspiring further study and inquiry. Appendices 1 and 2 provide resources for deeper study into many of these topics.

Get to Know Your Students

Teaching relies on personal relationships, so getting to know your students and creating caring communities are extremely important elements of culturally responsive and sustaining teaching. Researching the histories of the ethnicities represented in your classroom provides a broad context to family stories. However, students' cultural identities are complex and shaped by unique experiences. Hispanic children and families in the United States maintain a great diversity of cultural backgrounds depending on their country or countries of origin. Additionally, cultural diversity within one country of origin, for example Nicaragua or Guatemala, is vast, multiracial, and should not be homogenized. Moll emphasized that "students' learning is bound within larger contextual, historical, political, and ideological frameworks that affect students' lives" (Gonzalez et al., 2005, p. ix). Thus, knowing these histories, student experiences, and cultural identities can shape and deepen an understanding of the school community.

Get to Know Your Community

Learning is a social process and, as noted by Gonzalez et al. (2005), "We feel instruction must be linked to students' lives and the details of effective pedagogy should be linked to local histories and community contexts" (p. ix). Thus, reaching beyond the walls of the classroom to embrace the knowledge within the community can enrich and empower our students. For example, invite a culture bearer to share their musical expertise and heritage with the class. This could be a caregiver, a faculty or staff member at the school, or a local musician who might offer a connection to the repertoire in this book. Teachers can also initiate a family folk song project in which students record a family member singing a folk song that they share with their classroom community. This activity bridges home and school music and allows students to learn about each other's musical traditions. Over time, teachers can build a library of family folk songs to use in the classroom, with permission.

Environment

Students need to see, hear, and witness their cultures represented throughout the school, and the images and messages portrayed should accurately and appropriately reflect the community. According to Gay (2018), "Symbols are powerful conveyors of meaning" (p. 51) and should affirm student identities. View everything in your classroom with a critical lens, sensitive to how genders, cultures, and ethnicities are represented. Teaching manipulatives, classroom objects, and wall displays should accurately represent all histories and celebrate the diversity of the student body and beyond. For example, a large world map could be displayed with pins to indicate ancestry for each student's family. In addition, display maps showing Indigenous lands prior to colonization to recognize and honor their history before disruption.

Children's Books

Relevant children's books that complement the repertoire should be made available to students. Children begin forming ideas about their own and other people's racial identities at a very young age, making it imperative to include identity exploration in early childhood and elementary classrooms. High-quality multicultural children's books that are relevant to the children in your class can help develop positive racial identities and provide perspectives and stories for students outside of a culture. It is important to analyze children's literature for how ethnicity is addressed, as some books still include stereotyping. Gay (2018) states that "multicultural literature must be taught thoughtfully and critically, not merely as a form of cultural tourism in which it is showcased to students without any interpretive and reflective engagement" (p. 169). Children's literature can provide cultural context for the repertoire in this book (see Appendix 1 for a list).

Language

Language in the classroom can be a primary source of communication and can potentially foster inclusivity or alienate students. The classroom community should learn each other's preferred names, pronunciations, and pronouns at the beginning of the school year, as these are strong connections to personal identity.

The terms we use need to be accurate, and sometimes *Latinx*, *Hispanic*, and *Spanish* are misunderstood, misused, or used interchangeably. *Latinx* is a geography-based term that represents people with ancestry in Latin America, which are nations in the Americas that speak Latin-derived languages such as Spanish, Portuguese, and French. *Hispanic* is language-based and indicates that a person, culture, or country has Spanish-speaking heritage. Lastly, the term *Spanish* refers to nationality; if someone is Spanish, this means they are from Spain. While the identifiers Latinx and Hispanic are widely used, they have roots in colonialism and disregard Indigenous history and communities with languages and cultures other than those imposed by colonization. Historically, Latinos were conditioned to accept their Spanish heritage and deny African and Indigenous roots. However, recent identifiers have emerged such as *Afro-Latinx*, *Indigenous-Latinx*, and *Afro-Indigenous Latinx* to represent and embrace diverse heritages. When considering terms and identifiers, it is important to recognize the incredible diversity of culture groups under the umbrella of a single term and to avoid the homogenization of groups of people. It must also be noted that not everyone embraces these terms, and at the writing of this book the term *Latine* is used as an alternative to *Latinx*.

The terms *America* and *American*, which refer to all of North and South America, are also frequently misunderstood. Citizens of Guatemala and Nicaragua are Americans, and they are also *guatemaltecan* (Guatemalan) and *nicaragüense* (Nicaraguan). Citizens in the United States are also Americans, however, many people in the United States embrace this identifier as strictly their own, which can be found offensive or patronizing to people living outside of the United States. Other countries have terms to more appropriately define U.S. citizens, for example, the Spanish word *estadounidense* is defined as someone who is from the United States. The equivalent demonym in English is *United Statesian*, but this term is rarely used. Choosing a different grammar structure, however, one can simply say, "I am from the United States" to more accurately convey this geographical relationship.

Most languages can be assigned to one of three groups: (1) grammatical gendered languages (or gendered languages), which have nouns that are either masculine or feminine; (2) natural gender language, which distinguishes gender through pronouns (he and she) but nouns are not gendered; and (3) genderless languages, which lack grammatical gender distinction. The Spanish language is a grammatical gendered language, and research demonstrates that engaging in these languages influences our perceptions of gender and results in higher levels of sexism. Some Spanish speakers have proposed language changes to create a genderless language. For example, the term *Latinx* or *Latine* is used as a gender-neutral form of Latina/o. When teaching the repertoire in this book, be mindful of gender roles in singing games and the potential implications in your classroom community. Gender-neutral lyric suggestions are offered on the companion website for select songs in this collection.

With growing research and heightened awareness of teaching pedagogies and repertoire that alienate or harm students, we must reflect on our practice and make changes to create a more equitable learning environment. This call to action to improve our field to serve all of our students must be met not only with rigor but also with compassion and understanding. We are lifelong learners and should strive to improve all aspects of ourselves and our teaching, recognizing and learning from mistakes along the way. Challenging ourselves to improve our teaching can be difficult and uncertain, and can make us feel vulnerable or even inadequate. We must be gentle and forgiving yet demanding with ourselves and each other as we challenge the perceived safety of maintaining the status quo. After all, as attributed to Maya Angelou, "Do the best you can until you know better. Then when you know better, do better." We must all take active approaches to know better and to strive for justice in education.

Music in Central America

This chapter presents a history of music genres in Central America and chronicles Indigenous music and dance, the arrival of European music, and West African influence. An awareness of music history of the region frames the repertoire within a larger cultural context and can inform how this repertoire is presented to students.

Music in the Classic Mayan Period

Mayan civilization emerged and developed approximately between 200 BCE and 900 CE in what is now southern Mexico and Central America, reaching its peak in 800 CE and then suffering a steep decline. What we know about musical practices during this period comes from Spanish journals kept during initial and early contact with the Maya in the 1500s; archeological records such as stone murals, painted pottery, sculptures, and instruments made from ceramic and bone; and Mayan writings.

The Spanish burned most of the Mayan books, but four were preserved. Three were sent to Spain and were eventually discovered in the European cities for which they have since been named: the *Dresden Codex*, the *Codex Paris*, and the *Codex Madrid*. The fourth, the *Grolier Codex*, made its way to the United States and was exhibited at the Grolier Club in New York as part of a private collection. The *Grolier Codex* has since been renamed the *Maya Codex of Mexico*. These books, written in the 1100s on bark paper in Mayan hieroglyphics, referenced musical practices. Music traditions are also cited in *Los Cantares de Dzitbalché* (The Songs of Dzitbalché) and the *Popul Voh* (Book of Counsel), which were written after the conquest and contain history and mythology of the K'iche', one of the Mayan peoples. The cumulation of these artifacts has produced some knowledge of music culture during this period, but it is far from thorough.

The Maya constructed and played a variety of instruments. Percussion instruments included small vase-shaped pottery-framed drums (*kai yum*), waist-high wood-framed drums (*pax* or *zacatan*), two-tone drums made from hollowed logs (*tunkul*), turtle-shell drums, scrapers (*rascas*), rattles fashioned from gourds and shells, and small ankle bells made from gold and copper. Wind instruments included ocarinas, flutes made from clay, wood, or bone, and trumpets (*hom-tahs*) made out of wood, clay, gourds, or conch shells. Instruments were sometimes built in the shape of an animal or decorated with religious symbols that indicated the purposes of the music they were intended to accompany. Placed in the tombs of kings and priests, it was believed that instruments would ease the passage into the spirit world.

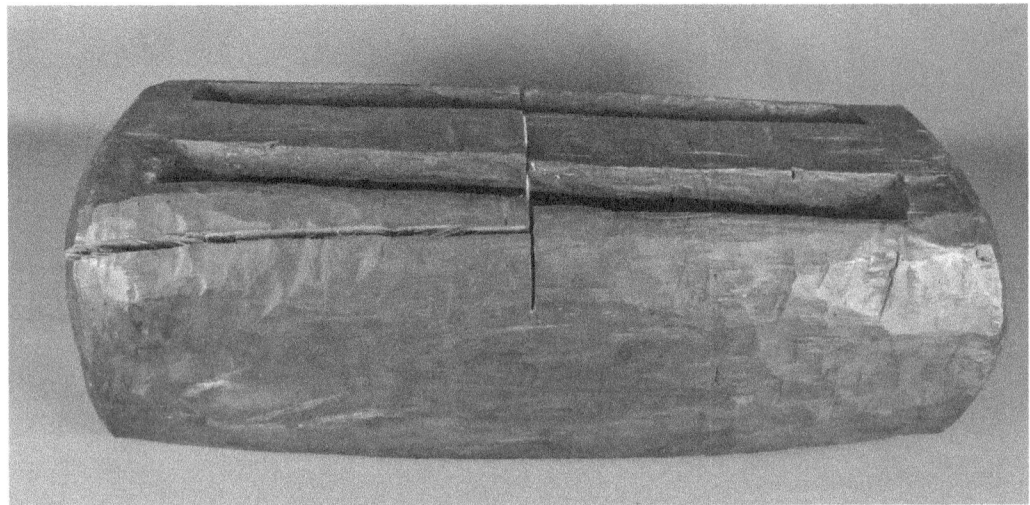

Tunkul (Courtesy of The Spurlock Museum, University of Illinois at Urbana-Champaign.)

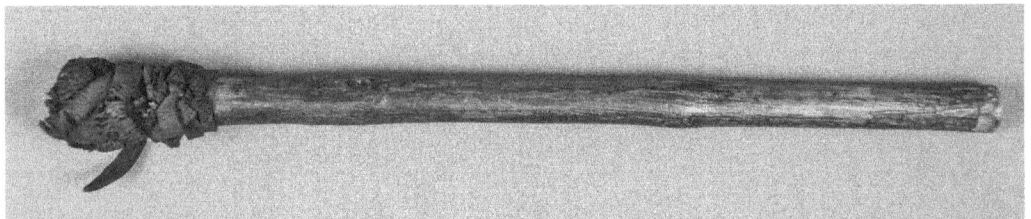

Tunkul beater (Courtesy of The Spurlock Museum, University of Illinois at Urbana-Champaign.)

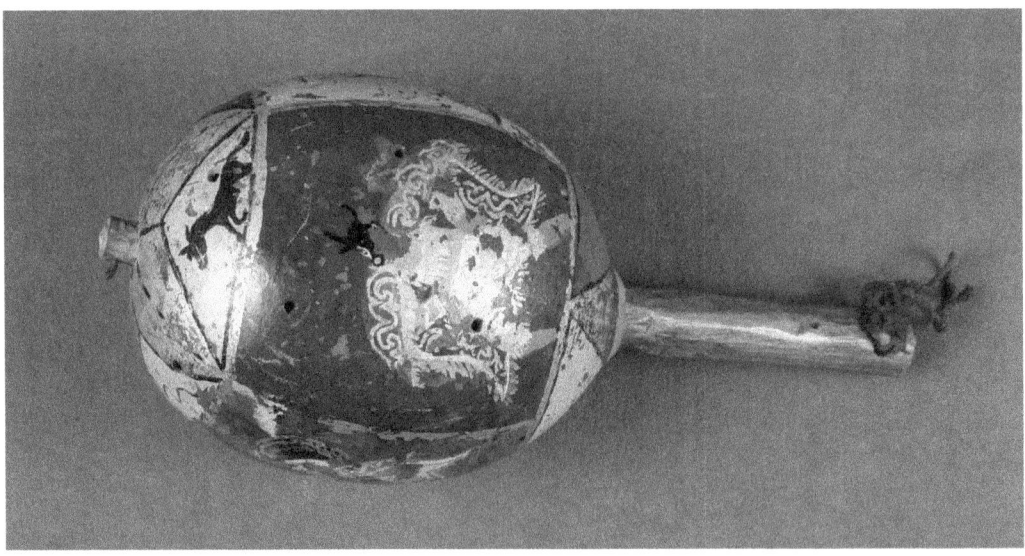

Rattle (Courtesy of The Spurlock Museum, University of Illinois at Urbana-Champaign.)

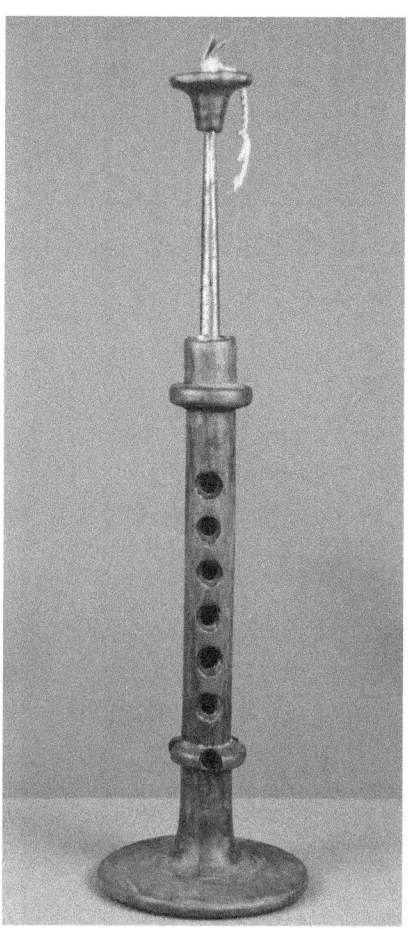

Flute (Courtesy of The Spurlock Museum, University of Illinois at Urbana-Champaign.)

Instrumental and singing practices were depicted in murals and illustrations, but no evidence of written melodies or rhythms has ever been discovered. Undoubtedly an oral tradition, Mayan music was either lost or endured with Spanish influences. The most intact musical genre in current practice is shamanic songs, which are performed by a shaman (*curandero*) during rituals, such as to bless homes and crops.

An essential part of daily life, music was used to communicate with the gods and was integrated into religious rituals, ceremonies, funerals, and warfare. Music provided entertainment and dance accompaniment, and held importance in orally preserving military, religious, and community history. Because of the value of music in Mayan life, musicians held an elevated position in society.

Dance Traditions

Dance-plays, now referred to as *bailes* (dances), incorporated music, dance, and drama and served several purposes in political, social, and religious life. The artform was used to communicate between tribes, announce war, tell stories, preserve history, and aid in healing, fertility, and hunting rituals. In Guatemala, many *bailes* are still performed today, such as *Danza de los venados* (Dance of the Deer), a pre-Hispanic dance that tells a story of deer hunting and the struggle between hunters and wild animals. *Danza de los monos* (Dance of the Monkeys) is based on a myth that is written in *Popul Voh* and tells the story of two brothers who were turned into monkeys due to jealousy of their older siblings. *Danze de los vaqueros* (Dance of the Cowboy) is about Spanish bullfighting.

When the Spanish arrived, they found it advantageous that the Maya had an established dance-play tradition and participated in this artform as a tactic to convert the Maya to Christianity. The conquistadors introduced new dances with persuasive themes to imply a superiority of European-Christian worldviews; dance themes suggested that if the Maya converted to European traditions they would be rewarded and accommodated by the Spanish. For example, *Danza de la conquista* (Dance of the Conquest) is about the death of the Mayan king Tecun Uman, who died in battle while fighting the Spanish. The final scene depicts the Indigenous people converting to Christianity and everyone dancing together in community and forgiveness. *Danza de moros y cristianos* (Dance of the Moors and Christians) retells the story of the Spanish struggle against the Arabs in their homeland, and Christianity is emphasized as the power that gave the Spanish an advantage in their struggle.

Similarly, historic dances are maintained in Nicaragua through cultural practices, such as *El güegüense* (Wise Man). A signature postcolonial folkloric dance, the name is derived from the word *huehue* from the Indigenous Nahuatl language in which it was originally performed. The satirical drama originated as street theater and mocks the Spanish and protests colonial rule. The dance *Palo de mayo* (Maypole) is celebrated in Afro-Caribbean communities on the east coast of Nicaragua, Belize, Honduras, and Panama, and pays tribute to the African goddess of fertility, Mayaya. These origins are debated; some claim that the tradition was adapted from a May Day dance brought by the British and others believe it comes from Jamaica. Dancing of the *Toro huaco* is featured at the Saint Sebastian festival in Diriamba. It tells the story of Indigenous hardships and hunger under Spanish rule that prompted them to steal cattle in the middle of the night under a full moon. The myth maintains that the perished cattle would come back to life and attack the hunters. ▶

Folkloric dance in Antigua, Guatemala (Photo by Rachel Gibson)

Spanish Music Influences

The Spanish brought Roman Catholic religious music to Central America, and Gregorian chant and sacred polyphony became part of the repertoire beginning in the 1500s. Chants, prayers, and religious music were used as a conversion tool for the Indigenous people to accept Spanish dominance and rule. Fearing that Indigenous music might aid in uprisings and rebellions, the Spanish suppressed Mayan music and dance practices by destroying their instruments and capturing musicians. However, this tactic was not always successful because the geographic reality of mountains, streams, and a long rainy season resulted in some Mayan groups having little to no contact with the Spanish, thus maintaining their traditions.

With the arrival of Spanish musicians to the colony, composers and musicians published and performed repertoire that included operas, masses, choral pieces, symphonic works, chamber music, and musical theater. Chapelmasters and organists were pillars of musical leadership in the church. For example, Hernando Franco (1532–1585) was the chapelmaster at the Guatemala Cathedral and the leading composer in the new colony. He was known to draw on both European and Indigenous themes in his music compositions.

The Spanish brought European instruments to the isthmus that were then replicated with Indigenous labor. The organ was the first instrument to be copied and other instruments soon followed, such as the guitar, harp, flute, flageolet, horn, coronet, bassoon, trombone, oboe, sackbut, dulcimer, and trumpet. Later to arrive were the violin, violincello, and the clarinet. Over time, these instruments, along with European scales and harmonic structures, were implemented in a variety of sacred and secular musical traditions in Central America, including military brass bands, processional music for celebrations, and vocal music accompanied by piano, harp, or guitar.

As Central American nations started gaining independence in the 1800s, and music became important to establishing national identities. Cultural centers, schools of music, and theaters were built to support and bolster the arts, and featured traditional European ensembles such as orchestras, chamber groups, choirs, and opera troupes.

The Marimba

Popular throughout Central America, the marimba has a long history in the region and is the national instrument of Guatemala, Nicaragua, and Costa Rica. The large handcrafted instrument consists of different-sized wooden bars that are struck with mallets, while gourds or wooden boxes serve as individual resonance chambers underneath to amplify the sound. The origins of the Central American marimba have long been debated. Evidence suggests that the enslaved African population in Central America recreated the marimbas of their homeland, which were later adopted by Indigenous communities. However, the African population in Central America was very small and did not remain as intact ethnic groups after mixing with the Indigenous and Indigenous-Spanish populations. Some speculate that the instrument's strong presence in the Indigenous communities and the lack of marimbas in the African population that later arrived on the Caribbean coast prove that it must have always been a traditional Mayan instrument. Others claim that Central Americans negated evidence of African origins to deny this part of their ancestry. Evidence does imply African origins, however, as the materials, structure, and building techniques all resemble its African counterpart. In addition, among the many depictions of instruments in Mayan art, there are no marimbas. Thus, it is more commonly accepted that the marimba is of African origin.

The Central American marimba has undergone changes specific to each nation over the last two centuries as modifications have been made to the size, shape, and available pitches. Marimba bands can be found throughout Central America as entertainment for street processionals, parties, festivals, and in hotels and restaurants. Alongside marimbas you might see guitars, harps, violins, or brass instruments. European-derived instruments have merged into the local traditions, resulting in many different ensemble configurations. The marimba is currently cherished and shared among both the Spanish-Indigenous and Mayan communities. ▶

Marimba band Orquesta Vozali at José Pingüino Restaurant in Panajachel, Guatemala (Photo by Rachel Gibson)

Nueva Canción

Nueva Canción, a folk genre and social movement that emerged in the 1970s and 1980s, featured beautifully sung melodies with lyrics meant to inspire and organize citizens to rally for causes of social justice and equality. A leading musician in this movement and the Nicaragua Revolution was Carlos Mejía Godoy. His music, which consciously integrated the diverse traditions of Nicaragua, reached a wide audience on the radio and was a voice of influence in the struggle for human rights. His songs contained courageous lyrics that supported the rebel fighters and commemorated the struggles of the poor. In 1972, he hosted a broadcast called *El son nuestro de cada día* (Our Song for Each Day), which circulated music and traditional antiauthoritarian folk tales to criticize the military dictatorship in Nicaragua.

Contributing to the Nueva Canción genre, the musical group Duo Guardabarranco—Salvador Cardenal Barquero (b. 1960) and his sister Katia Cardenal (b. 1963)—began performing in 1980. Their beautiful folk melodies embraced an international pop character as they consciously avoided traditional sounds of Nicaragua in the hope that their messages of peace and social justice might reach a global audience. They wrote and shared music about the economically marginalized, importance of freedom, and a respect for nature. They became one of the most important music groups to represent Nicaragua as they spread messages of peace, justice, and hope through their music.

Garifuna Music

Garifuna music and dance practices belong to the Garinagu, a culture group exiled to the Honduran coast in the 1700s from the island of St. Vincent in the Caribbean. They are descended from West Africans and Amerindian Arawaks and currently reside along the Caribbean coast of Nicaragua, Honduras, Guatemala, and Belize, in addition to a diaspora of 100,000 individuals in the United States. They share a common language that is primarily based on Arawak but incorporates elements of European and African languages. The most popular music performed by this group is the *Punta*, a dance-song genre that is a symbolic representation of the cock-and-hen mating dance. Traditionally performed as a couples dance, it features rapid movement of the buttocks and hips while maintaining a motionless torso. The dance is accompanied by call–response singing and rhythmic instrumentation of drums, rattles, and conch shell trumpets. Once deemed inappropriate for children due to the explicit gestures, the dance evolved and was modified to represent and express the hardships and joys of life. It is now integrated into holidays, celebrations, and rituals. These changes prompted youth participation and the inclusion of female drummers and musicians, who once were banned from playing the instrumentation. Punta Rock developed in the 1980s–1990s and is a modern adaptation influenced by Punta and *Paranda*, a folk genre for guitar and voice. Very popular with teenagers and adults, Punta Rock affirms and celebrates Garinagu identity.

Miskitu Music

The Indigenous Miskitu people reside on the Caribbean coast in Nicaragua, Honduras, and Costa Rica, where they remained autonomous from the Spanish conquest and thus maintained their language, music, dance, and other cultural traditions. Historically a native American group, they have mixed with Europeans and Africans over the last five centuries, which has influenced their cultural expressions and artforms. The Miskitu language is spoken as well as Miskitu Coast Creole and Spanish. Music is integrated into ritual practices by shamans and used for secular entertainment, the most popular being *kitarlawana*, a term that originates from *kitar* (guitar) and *lawana* (song). Typically composed by men, the six-string (or less) lute accompanies a sung melody about longing for women or other themes. The functional harmony of these songs demonstrates the European influence on this genre of music. Other instruments might add additional accompaniment, for example *tina*, a washtub base with one string, *kuswa taya*, a tortoise shell that produces two tones when struck, and *aras napat*, a scraper instrument made out of a horse jaw.

Current Music Traditions

Music and dance imports from neighboring regions have corresponded with the rise of mass media, music industries, and electronic communications. Salsa from New York City, bachata and merengue from Brazil, and mariachi from Mexico spread throughout the region and are popular forms of dance and music entertainment frequently enjoyed in restaurants, bars, and in the streets. As personal sound systems in homes have become more common, reggae from Jamaica, reggaeton from Panama, cumbia from Colombia, calypso and soca from Trinidad and Tobago, and rock, hip-hop, metal, hardcore, punk, and singer-songwriting from the United States have influenced music traditions in Central America.

Shaped by history, a rich variety of music thrives in Central America and is maintained in families and communities. Indigenous, African-derived, European, international popular music, and children's music all exist and will give rise to new traditions as upcoming generations chart a new musical future.

A Brief History of Central America

The history of Central America directly impacts current events, and exploring the social, political, and economic reasons why Guatemalans and other Central Americans emigrate to the United States deepens our connections to family stories and legacies. This chapter offers a brief overview of the region.

The earliest known civilization in Central America was developed by the Olmecs (1500 BCE), who constructed cities in the fertile river areas of the southern gulf coast of what is now Mexico. After the collapse of the Olmecs (300 BCE), subsequent civilizations emerged and declined: Maya (200 BCE– 900 CE), Teotihuacan (c. 200–550 CE), Toltec (c. 900–1168 CE), and Aztec (1345–1521 CE). All boasted major accomplishments in writing, astronomy, architecture, and art. The Maya would become one of the world's most advanced civilizations of its time, and by 300 BCE 14 million inhabitants lived in cities, villages, and the countryside, making it one of the largest population centers in the world at the time. While it is not certain why the Mayan civilization collapsed, it is thought to have been caused by any combination of natural catastrophes, overpopulation, and war. Although this resulted in the abandonment of cities, the Mayas themselves and their cultural and socioeconomic practices persisted, and approximately 10 million live in the same region today.

Ancient Maya city Tikal in Flores, Petén, Guatemala

The Spanish began exploring the area in 1502 and commented on the sophistication and size of the abandoned cities. In 1510, Vasco Núñez de Balboa created the first European settlement, Santa María la Antigua, in what is now Panama. This marked the beginning of what would be a devastating 300-year period of colonization that attempted to erase Indigenous culture and forever changed the land and livelihood they had known for hundreds of years. The conquistadors' ability to dominate the areas with which they came into contact relied on Indigenous allies and a population weakened or diminished by diseases to which the local population had no immunity. Spain claimed the region after much death and destruction, and by the mid-1500s the empire was named the Kingdom of Guatemala.

The Spanish decided on governmental configurations, borders, and capitals while coerced Indigenous labor built the infrastructure.[1] Each Spanish town featured a central square with a church and official buildings, surrounded by a grid of perpendicular streets for stores and homes. These sites were deliberately located where there was access to Indigenous populations that could be forced into labor and converted to Catholicism. The mountainous topography did allow some Mayan communities to experience little to no contact with the Spanish, such as the Guatemalan Highlands

---

1 While the Spanish imperial system was to some degree based on earlier practices developed during the Reconquista, the conquest of Muslim kingdoms in the south of Spain that happened over centuries, it is important to note that the colonial system was built on an Indigenous foundation in the major population centers, such as Guatemala. Labor practices, such as encomienda, depended on existing requirements of average Mayas providing annual labor duties to their state. Spanish administrators relied on local Indigenous leaders to enforce compliance with Spanish labor demands. Thus, the imperial system in the more central areas of Mexico, Central America, and the central Andes saw significant survival of preconquest forms of political and economic organization.

and southern and western Yucatan. These groups were fortunate enough to remain on or near the ancestral land that defined their identities for generations, and they maintained their politics, religion, culture, and economic organization long after the conquest. However, the majority of the Indigenous population suffered greatly at the hands of the Spanish conquistadores and died in great numbers from overwork, starvation, and diseases. Many who survived were forced into slavery. The Indigenous population declined by 90 percent across the region, which is often cited as one of the worst demographic disasters in world history. Without sufficient Indigenous labor to build infrastructure, the Spanish made a decision to purchase slaves, a practice that resulted in 30,000 enslaved Africans on the isthmus.

By 1620, there were 15,000 Spaniards living in 15 towns, the largest being Granada, San Salvador, and Comayagua. Few women from Spain came to live in Central America and the Spanish partnered with Indigenous women to create a new ethnic group whose population eventually dominated most large cities throughout Central America. From the beginning of the conquest and reaching near obsession by the 1700s, the Spanish government attempted to create and enforce a caste system. Spaniards were at the top of this hierarchy and Africans and the Indigenous groups made up the bottom ranks. In part, this was in response to a demographic rebound as the Indigenous population was growing again after centuries of decline.

Even though Indigenous people made up 80 percent of the population, they were exploited, had few to no rights, and worked for the Spanish under conditions that left them perpetually in debt. The Spanish (and later regimes of the 1800s) constructed a variety of mechanisms to force the Mayas out of the protected highlands to the lowland plantations. Debt peonage ensured easy access to a cheap labor source, a practice that continued on banana plantations in the 1900s. These unjust labor practices created conflicts and confrontations that eventually led to revolts against the Spanish.

Spain was dissatisfied with the colony, as they evaluated its success based on financial rewards. Without the major deposits of silver and large population centers that offered cheap and easy access to Indigenous labor, such as in Mexico and Peru, Central America remained a financial disappointment for much of the 300 years of colonization. As a result, friction developed and the citizens of the Kingdom of Guatemala became increasingly aware of the surrounding wars for independence to the north and south. Colombia (including Panama) fought and ultimately gained independence from Spain in 1819, and Mexico gained its freedom in 1821. While movements for independence in the provinces of Central America were often disjointed and sporadic, success came briefly in 1821 but was destroyed the following year when Central America was forced to accept incorporation into Mexico. In 1823, Central America declared independence from Mexico and established itself as the Federal Republic of Central America. However, this unity dissolved into civil war by 1840, and the region has since experienced periods of regional solidarity and more localized nationalism. They decided on the political structure of the United Provinces of Central America, which consisted of a federal capital in Guatemala City and five autonomous states, each with its own president: Guatemala, El Salvador, Honduras, Nicaragua, and Costa Rica. (Belize theoretically remained part of Guatemala even though the British occupied its coastal regions; Panama was part of Colombia.)

Throughout the mid-1800s, foreigners intruded on the isthmus and forever changed Central America. Britain seized the Nicaraguan port of San Juan del Norte and dominated the Indigenous Miskitu population and to land on the Caribbean coast. Investors from the United States, such as Cornelius Vanderbilt, constructed railroads in Nicaragua and Panama and facilitated commercial shipping across the Atlantic and Pacific Oceans. This made it possible for Central American countries to pursue large-scale export economies in coffee, which became its main export crop starting in 1870. By the late 19th century, much of Central America existed under dictatorships or oligarchic democracy, following the tenets of classical liberalism. Lauding the sacred right and value of private property as the path to modernity, land was seized from the church and Indigenous populations and redistributed to the Spanish and foreign investors to increase coffee production. As these exports increased, labor shortages occurred; Central American governments responded with a variety of mechanisms to coerce the poor to work the coffee plantations for little pay.[2] (Only Costa Rica, with its system of family farms, was able to avoid this exploitation.) Over time, wages declined, malnutrition increased, and the poor rebelled against the land owners and their abusive practices. The presence of the military intimidated the workers and prohibited uprisings. By the late 1800s, coffee growers maintained a great deal of power and wealth in the Central American nations and maintained much of this control into the 21st century.

Central America started exporting bananas in 1870, and U.S. robber barons invested in the building of railroads to make this commercial export possible. Land was awarded to North American companies, such as the United Fruit Company, for these infrastructure investments, and by 1910 they owned 80 percent of the banana crop and the best lands on the Caribbean coast, thus maintaining much power in the region. For example, Honduras was the world's largest banana producer from 1925 to 1939, but remained sadly underdeveloped. In Guatemala, a nation where 90 percent of the exports were either coffee or bananas, only 2.2 percent of the population owned 70 percent of the land. These practices created a large class of underpaid and powerless rural workers.

Many changes occurred in Central America in the early 1900s. The area experienced modernization and growth in education programs and there was at least one university and library in each republic. Developments were also made in health services and sanitation, which resulted in a population increase. In spite of modernization, there were still

---

2   There were many different methods that were used in the 19th and 20th centuries to extract labor from the Mayan population and other subjugated groups throughout Central America. Vagrancy laws required all peasants to demonstrate having worked for wages for a specific number of days, and they were required to carry a kind of passport with stamps to prove that labor (usually on a banana or coffee plantation). Any peasant who could not prove this was summarily arrested and deposited on the nearest plantation to work. Debt peonage also continued throughout this period.

few opportunities for social mobility other than joining the military. Poverty was ubiquitous (particularly in rural areas since the new modern services were almost exclusively in urban zones). Foreign interests controlled the natural resources, owned the infrastructure and the best agricultural land, and dominated port facilities. This all translated into raw political power as they dictated to weak and unstable Central American governments. By the early 1900s, the United States was a dominant force in Central American commerce, which continued to grow with the help of local dictators.

As U.S. investments in Central America increased in the second half of the 19th century, so did the interest of the U.S. government in the political and economic stability of the region. By 1900 most Central American nations were ruled by dictators, in many cases aided by the intervention of the U.S. military. These regimes suppressed free speech, censored the press, and imposed martial law. Political corruption was endemic and the military expanded, which resulted in frequent coups d'état. The chronic social unrest worried the foreign businesses and their governments because profits depended on stable exploitation of a poor and vulnerable rural laboring class. To ensure consistent access to a cheap, large labor pool, the U.S. government and its powerful economic interests were increasingly involved in the politics of the region. Through a variety of different foreign policy doctrines, including McKinley's and Roosevelt's Gunboat Diplomacy, Taft's Dollar Diplomacy, and later, Truman's Doctrine of Containment, the U.S. Department of State rationalized decades of military interventions and invasions and extended occupations in the Caribbean and Central America. Eventually, in nations like Guatemala and Honduras, U.S. corporations owned more of the economy than the local population. With increasing power in Central America and in the world, the United States completed the Panama Canal in 1914 for its navy and further economic gain.

Increased U.S. intervention in Central America generated strong resentment and nationalistic fervor on the part of the citizens. They noted the success of the Mexican Revolution (1910–1917) in ousting the country of its dictator and instituting progressive social policies. This awareness prompted strikes in Central America, the first of which started in Honduras on the United Fruit Company banana plantations in 1917. However, these uprisings were quickly shattered by the military. Over time, this unrest instigated a more organized resistance movement rooted in a nationalistic backlash to U.S. presence. In the 1920s, Augusto César Sandino led a resistance movement in Nicaragua with a peasant army using guerilla tactics to protest U.S. military occupation and control of the customs office of the Nicaraguan government. The U.S. government ultimately withdrew its troops in 1933 at the request of the Nicaraguan government, but only after the U.S. Marines had established and trained the U.S.-allied Nicaraguan National Guard. Originally intended to be an apolitical professional army/police force, it became the greatest source of repression and violence against the Nicaraguan people for more than 40 years. This wave of nationalism was not limited to Nicaragua.

Following urban uprisings in Guatemala's cities in 1944, the dictatorship of Jorge Ubico was finally eliminated and Guatemalans experienced the first free and honest elections in the nation's history. The revolutionary government, which only lasted until 1954, promised reforms to lift the country out of poverty and underdevelopment. However, Jacobo Arbenz's efforts to institute land reforms in the early 1950s threatened the monopoly on power that the United Fruit Company had worked so hard to achieve and maintain since the late 1800s. Confronting a Guatemalan government no longer willing to put its needs first, the United Fruit Company turned to the U.S. government when some of its land was expropriated, claiming the revolutionary government was communist. In the polarized world of the Cold War, implementing land reform was tantamount to declaring war on the United States, whose Central Intelligence Agency (CIA) was given the mission of creating a counterrevolutionary "army" to topple Arbenz. He was driven into exile by a CIA propaganda campaign, attacked by the Roman Catholic Church from every pulpit in Guatemala, and experienced powerful pressure exerted by the U.S. State Department in the Organization of American States and the United Nations. In spite of claims that U.S. intervention represented the protection of freedom and democracy, in the decades following the coup Guatemala became the site of the worst human rights abuses in all of Latin America.

Throughout the Cold War, the governments of Honduras, El Salvador, and Nicaragua were dominated by military or personalistic dictatorships. What elections existed were typically meaningless exercises intended to create a veneer of democracy to ensure continued financial assistance from the United States, thus, these governments received millions every year in U.S. military aid. The Alliance for Progress was implemented by John F. Kennedy with the intention of avoiding armed revolution by instituting incremental reforms to alleviate the extreme poverty in the region. However, this was ultimately a failure, as Lyndon B. Johnson shifted an increasing amount of the funds away from economic development and toward military aid. This assistance also included increasing numbers of Latin American military officers being trained at the School of the Americas located in the Panama Canal Zone and later at Fort Benning, Georgia. This school trained the officers to ensure "internal security" in the region, which was a Cold War euphemism for the repression of dissent and dismantling of human rights organizations, unions, and other reform movements.

A population explosion in the 1960s and 1970s forced many to migrate to cities to find work, and areas in Central America that were once almost entirely rural were transformed into overpopulated urbanized regions. This shift created tremendous economic and political instability. There was little employment, housing, education, or other means of survival available. Urban reform movements were violently crushed by the militaries of these nations; those who supported the most basic improvements, such as clean water or free speech, were arrested, tortured, and sometimes disappeared. In response to this repression, rural guerrilla armies emerged in El Salvador, Guatemala, and Nicaragua. In 1979, the Sandinista National Liberation Front (FSLN), named for the nationalist hero of the 1920s Augusto César Sandino, was able to overthrow the Somoza regime after 43 years of rule, which was the only revolutionary movement able to triumph in Central

America. During its 10 years in power, the FSLN government (commonly known as the Sandinistas) was able to make tremendous gains in education, health services, and the arts. In spite of maintaining a nonaligned foreign policy and a mixed economy, the Reagan administration labeled this government communist and built an army of exiles called the Contras to destroy the FSLN government, repeating the CIA strategy of 1954. In spite of the Boland Amendment, which forbade any aid to overthrow a government with which the United States was not at war, officials in the Reagan administration continued to funnel money and weapons to the Contras using funds derived from illegal arms sales to Iran. Known as the Iran-Contra Affair, the weapons were delivered on planes that also trafficked cocaine for Colombian drug lords. Peace talks resulted in elections in 1990, during which the United States remained steadfast in its support of the Contras until the Sandinistas were removed from power. After 17 years of neoliberal presidents, Nicaragua restored the FSLN leader Daniel Ortega to the presidency in 2007. He remains the president in 2021, but not without controversy.

El Salvador was engaged in a Civil War (1979–1992) that was fought between the Farabundo Martí National Liberation Front (FMLN) and the military-led government. Similarly, with the perceived threat of rising communism in Central America, the United States sent aid to support the military in El Salvador. Although the FMLN was able to occupy and govern large sections of northern El Salvador, they were unable to take the capital and ended in a stalemate with the sham democratic government of José Napoleon Duarte. The Chapultepec Peace Accords were signed in 1992, which held peaceful hopes for the citizens.

Civil war in Guatemala (1960–1996) was similarly fought by the leftist rebel groups consisting of the marginalized lower class and Mayas who were intent on overthrowing the military dictatorship that prevented electoral politics. With scorched-earth policy as the norm, the government committed genocide against the Mayas and burned entire villages to the ground, claiming they were guerrilla sympathizers aiding in the revolt against the government. Despite international criticism of the Guatemalan government, the U.S. government continued sending economic and military aid, which supported their efforts. After causing the deaths of more than 70,000 civilians during his 14 months as president of Guatemala, Efraín Ríos Montt was described by President Reagan as getting a "bum rap" on human rights. But just as the end of the Cold War had eliminated much of the rationale for supporting the dictatorship of El Salvador as public opinion became increasingly critical of U.S. policy, the U.S. government also supported the Guatemalan Peace Accord, signed in 1996, which set out peaceful goals for the country.

The effects of the civil wars in Central America were and continue to be devastating to its citizens. Approximately 300,000 lost their lives and two million became refugees and fled to Mexico, Belize, Costa Rica, Panama, and the United States. The economy suffered greatly and democratic elections were welcomed in the region by the 1990s from a population that was weary of war and unjust governmental practices.

Remarkable achievements were made in Central America in the 1990s as peace, democracy, and civil rights emerged to empower many who had been oppressed. These changes prompted a cultural resurgence of marginalized groups such as the Maya, and policies were set in place to address issues of discrimination and social justice. By the 2000s, the difficulties inherent in advancing these gains had become evident. The democratization of the isthmus had yet to eliminate political abuses, corruption, or violence. While demilitarization was a marked advancement toward peace, issues of safety, gangs, and international drug trafficking are still a public threat. Poverty and social inequities are persistent issues, and during these first years of peace, half of Central Americans are living in abject poverty. New economic undertakings and efforts to correct the abuses of the past may eventually bring about a more prosperous and stronger Central America. While much still remains to be accomplished, efforts toward peace and stability have resulted in an emerging tourism industry that attracts international visitors to cities, towns, universities, language schools, and cultural heritage sites.

APPENDIX 1
Resources: Literature

Classroom Resources: Children's Books

Elementary Literature

Berlak, A. (2015). *Joelito's big decision / La gran decisión de Joelito*. Hard Ball Press.

Bernier-Grand, C. T. (2004). *César: ¡Sí, se puede! / Yes, we can!* Marshall Cavendish.

Brown, M. (2013). *Tito Puente, Mambo king / Rey de Mambo*. Harper Collins.

Buitrago, J. (2017). *Walk with me / Camino a casa*. Groundwood Books.

Gonzalez, X. (2017). *All around us*. Cinco Puntos Press.

Lacámara, L. (2017). *Dalia's wondrous hair*. Arte Publico Press.

Lui-Trujillo, R. (2015). *Furqan's first flat top*. Come Bien Books.

Martinez-Neal, J. (2018). *Alma y como obtuvo su nombre*. Candlewick Press.

Menchú, R. (2002). *The honey jar*. Groundwood Books.

Mills, D., & Alva, A. (2018). *La frontera: El viaje con papa / My journey with Papá*. Barefoot Books.

Morales, Y. (2016). *Little night nochecita*. Macmillan.

Morales, Y. (2018). *Dreamers*. Holiday House.

Otheguy, E. (2017). *Mart's song for freedom / Martí y sus versos por la libertad*. Children's Book Press.

Quintera, I. (2019). *My Papi has a motorcycle*. Penguin Books.

Tonatuih, D. (2013). *Pancho rabbit and the coyote: A migrant's tale*. Harry N. Abrams.

Tonatuih, D. (2014). *Separate is never equal: Sylvia Mendez and her family fight for desegregation*. Harry N. Abrams.

Weatherford, C. B. (2017). *Schomberg: The man who built a library*. Candlewick Press.

Middle School Literature

Ada, A. F. (1998). *Under the royal palms*. Atheneum Books for Young Readers.

Agosín, M. (2015). *I lived on butterfly hill*. Simon & Schuster.

Alvaréz, J. (2010). *Return to sender*. Random House.

Argueta, J. (2019). *Caravan to the north: Misael's long walk*. Groundwood Books.

Brown, S. (2014). *Caminar*. Candlewick Press.

Cartaya, P. (2017). *The epic fail of Arturo Zamora*. Penguin Books.

Conkling, W. (2011). *Sylvia and Aki.* Tricycle Press.

Elliot, Z. (2014). *¡Max loves muñecas!* Createspace Independent Publishing.

Engle, M. (2014). *Silver people: Voices from the Panama Canal.* Houghton Mifflin Harcourt.

Engle, M. (2018). *Forest world.* Atheneum Books for Young Readers.

Menchu. R., & Liano, D. (2005). *The girl from Chimel.* Groundwood Books.

Peréz, C. (2017). *The first rule of punk.* Penguin Books.

Torres, J. (2017). *Stef Soto, taco queen.* Hachette Book Group.

Young Adult and Adult Literature

Belli, G. (2003). *Country under my skin: A memoir of love and war.* Anchor Books.

Brignoli, H. P. (1989). *Brief history of Central America.* University of California Press.

Cardoza, M. (2016). *13 colors of the Honduran resistance.* CreateSpace.

Dario, R. (1888). *Azul.* BN Publishing.

Euraque, D., & Martinez, Y. (2016). *The African diaspora in educational programs of Central America.*

Gleijeses, P. (1992). *Shattered hope: The Guatemalan revolution and the United States 1944–1954.* Princeton University Press.

Gonzalez, J. (2011). *Harvest of empire: History of Latinos in America.* Penguin Books.

Grandin, G. (2000). *The blood of Guatemala: A history of race and nation.* Duke University Press.

Menchu, R. (1987). *I, Rigoberta Menchu: An Indian woman in Guatemala.* Verso Books.

Menchu. R. (1998). *Crossing borders.* Verso Books.

Menchu. R. (2008). *The secret legacy.* Groundwood Books.

Menchu. R. (2012). *K'aslemalil-Vivir: El caminar de Rigoberta Menchú Tum en el tiempo.* Universidad Nacional Autónoma de México.

Menjivar, C. (2005). *When states kill: Latin America, the U.S., and technologies of terror.* University of Texas Press.

Ramírez, S. (2007). *Adios muchachos: A memoir of the Sandanista revolution.* Duke University Press.

Rodriguez, A. P. (2009). *Dividing the isthmus: Central American transnational histories, literatures, and cultures.* University of Texas Press.

Tobar, H. (2017). *The wandering song: Central American writing in the United States.* Tia Chucha.

Villalobos, J. P. (2019). *The other side: Stories of Central American teen refugees who dream of crossing the border.* Farrar, Straus, & Giroux.

Wilkinson, D. (2004). *Silence on the mountain: Stories of terror, betrayal, and forgetting in Guatemala.* Duke University Press.

For a full and updated book list, see the Social Justice Books Teaching for Change Project webpage for Central America. https://socialjusticebooks.org/booklists/central-ame

APPENDIX 2
Resources: Documentaries and Films

Travel
Miller, M. M. (Director). (2014). *Poverty, Inc.* [Film]. Michael Matheson Miller.

Mayan Culture and History
Engle, D. G. (Director). (2012). *Mayan Renaissance* [Film]. PeaceJam Production.

Guatemala
Clark, B. (Director). (2008). *Guatemala: The secret files* [Film]. Public Broadcasting Service, Frontline.

Engle, D. (1999). *Daughter of the Maya* [Film]. PeaceJam Production.

Nava, G. (Director). (1983). *El Norte* [Film]. Anna Thomas.

Rumph, T. (Director). (2008). *Voice of a mountain* [Film]. Hit & Run Productions.

Suffern, R. (Director). (2016). *Finding Oscar* [Film]. Ryan Suffer & Frank Marshall.

Yates, P. (Director). (1983). *When the mountains tremble* [Film]. Skylight Pictures.

Yates, P. (Director). (2011). *Granito* [Film]. Skylight Pictures.

Nicaragua
Littin, M. (Director). (1982). *Alsino y el Condor* [Film]. Instituto Nicaragüense de Cine.

El Salvador
Mondoki, L. (Director). (2004). *Voces Inocentes* [Film]. Lawrence Bender Production.

Zamora, M. (Director). (2015). *El cuarto de los huesos* [Film]. Sandía Digital.

WORKS CITED

Angelou, M. [@DrMayaAngelou]. (2018, August 12). *Do the best you can until you know better. Then when you know better, do better.* [Tweet]. Twitter. https://twitter.com/drmayaangelou/status/1028663286512930817?lang=en

Gay, G. (2018). *Culturally responsive teaching: Theory, research, and practice.* Teachers College Press.

González, N., Moll, L. C., & Amanti, C. (Eds.). (2005). *Funds of knowledge: Theorizing practices in households, communities, and classrooms.* Lawrence Erlbaum.

Kinloch, V. (2017). "You ain't making me write": Culturally sustaining pedagogies and black youths' performances of resistance. In D. Paris & H. S. Alim (Eds.), *Culturally sustaining pedagogies: Teaching and learning for justice in a changing world* (pp. 25–42). Teachers College Press.

Ladson-Billings, G. (1994). *The dreamkeepers: Successful teaching of African-American students.* Jossey-Bass.

Ladson-Billings, G. (1995). Toward a theory of culturally relevant pedagogy. *American Educational Research Journal, 32*(3), 465–491.

Lee, T. S., & McCarty, T. L. (2017). Upholding Indigenous education sovereignty through critical culturally sustaining/revitalizing pedagogy. In D. Paris & H. S. Alim (Eds.), *Culturally sustaining pedagogies: Teaching and learning for justice in a changing world* (pp. 61–82). Teachers College Press.

Paris, D., & Alim, H. S. (Eds.). (2017). *Culturally sustaining pedagogies: Teaching and learning for justice in a changing world.* Teachers College Press.

BIBLIOGRAPHY

Banks, J. A. (2003). *Handbook of research on multicultural education*. Jossey-Bass.

Banks, J. A., & McGee Banks, C. A. (Eds.). (2019). *Multicultural education: Issues and perspectives*. Wiley.

Barry, T., & Preush, D. (1986). *The Central America fact book*. Grove Press.

Béhague, G. (1979). *Music in Latin America: An introduction*. Prentice-Hall.

Brill, M. (2012). *Music of the ancient Maya: New avenues of research*. American Musicological Society.

Brown-Jeffy, S., & Cooper, J. E. (2011). Toward a conceptual framework of culturally relevant pedagogy: An overview of the conceptual of conceptual and theoretical literature. *Teacher Education Quarterly, 38*(1), 65–84.

Carrasco, D. (Ed.). (2001). Music. In *The Oxford encyclopedia of MesoAmerican cultures: The civilizations of Mexico and Central America* (pp. 356–358). Oxford University Press.

Chase, G. (1962). *A guide to the music of Latin America*. AMS Press.

Coatsworth, J. H. (1994). *Central America and the United States: The clients and the colossus*. Twayne Publishers.

Collins, B. A. (2014). Dual language development of Latino children: Effect of instructional program type and the home and school language environment. *Early Childhood Research Quarterly, 29*(3), 389–397.

Dominguez, M. (2017). "Se hace puentes al andar": Decolonial teacher education as a needed bridge to culturally sustaining and revitalizing pedagogies. In D. Paris & H. S. Alim (Eds.), *Culturally sustaining pedagogies: Teaching and learning for justice in a changing world* (pp. 225–246). Teachers College Press.

Foster, L. V. (2007). *A brief history of Central America*. Checkmark Books.

Garfias, R. (1983). The marimba of Mexico and Central America. *Latin America Music Review, 4*(2), 203–208.

Green, O. N. (2020). Ethnicity, modernity, and retention in the Garifuna Punta. *Black Music Research Journal, 22*(2), 189–216.

Howell, M. (2009). Music syncretism in the postclassic K'iche' warrior dance and the colonial period Baile de los Moros y Cristianos. In L. G. Cecil & T. W. Pugh (Eds.), *Maya worldviews at conquest* (pp. 279–298). University Press of Colorado.

Immerman, R. (1982). *The CIA in Guatemala*. University of Texas Press.

Kraus, C. (1991). *Inside Central America: Its people, politics, and history*. Summit Books.

LaFeber, W. (1993). *Inevitable revolutions* (2nd ed.). W. W. Norton.

Lind, V. R., & McKoy, C. (2016). *Culturally responsive teaching in music education: From understanding to application*. Routledge.

Merriam, A. P. (1964). *The anthropology of music*. Northwestern University Press.

Moreno, D. (1994). *The struggle for peace in Central America*. University Press of Florida.

Nettl, B. (2005). *The study of ethnomusicology: Thirty-one issues and concepts*. University of Illinois Press.

Olsen, D. A., & Sheehy, D. E. (1998). *The Garland encyclopedia of world music: Vol. 2. South America, Mexico, Central America, and the Caribbean*. Routledge.

Paris, D. (2012). Culturally sustaining pedagogy: A needed change in stance, terminology, and practice. *Educational Researcher*, *41*(3), 93–97.

Prewitt-Freilino, J., Caswell, T. A., & Laakso, E. (2012). The gendering of languages: A comparison of gender equality in countries gendered, natural gender, and genderless languages. *Sex Roles*, *66*(3–4), 268–281.

Ruz, M. H. (1994). Maya resistance to colonial rule in everyday life. *Latin America Anthropology Review*, *6*(1), 33–40.

Scruggs, T. M. (1999). Central America: Marimba and other musics of Guatemala and Nicaragua. In J. M. Schechter (Ed.), *Music in Latin American culture: Regional traditions* (pp. 80–125). Schirmer Books.

Scruggs, T. M. (1999). "Let's enjoy as Nicaraguans": The use of music in the construction of a Nicaraguan national consciousness. *Ethnomusicology*, *43*(2), 297–321.

Sharer, R. J. (1996). *Daily life in Maya civilization*. Greenwood Press.

Smith, S. M. (1948). *The history and use of music in colonial Spanish America 1500–1750* (Master's thesis, Loyola University Chicago). https://ecommons.luc.edu/luc_theses/808

Schechter, J. M. (1999). Themes in Latin American music culture. In J. M. Schechter (Ed.), *Music in Latin American culture: Regional traditions* (pp. 1–33). Schirmer Books.

Sturman, J. L. (2012). Nostalgia for the future: The new song movement in Nicaragua. In W. H. Beezley & L. A. Curcio-Nagy (Eds.), *Latin American popular culture since independence: An introduction* (2nd ed., pp. 247–266). Rowman & Littlefield.

Tenenbaum, B. A., & Dorn, G. M. (Eds.). (1996). Music. In *Encyclopedia of Latin American history and culture* (Vol. 4, pp. 135–149). C. Scribner's Sons.

Trehub, S. E., & Schellenburg, E. G. (1995). Music: Its relevance to infants. *Annals of Child Development*, *11*, 1–24.

Trehub, S. A., & Trainor, L. J. (1998). Singing to infants: Lullabies and play songs. *Advances in Infancy Research*, *12*, 43–77.

Trevarthen, C. (1999). Musicality and the intrinsic motive pulse: Evidence from human psychobiology and infant communication. *Musicae scientiae*. *3*(1_suppl), 155–215.

United States Central Intelligence Agency. (1982). *Central America* [Map]. https://www.loc.gov/item/2011586138/

Volk, T. M. (2004). *Music, education, and multiculturalism: Foundations and principles*. Oxford University Press.

Ward, C. (2017). *The family folk song project*. GIA Publications.

Wasserman, B. D., & Weselay, A. J. (2009). ¿Qué? Quoi? Do languages with grammatical gender promote sexist attitudes? *Sex Roles*, *61*(9), 634–643.

INDEX: SOURCES: SITES AND SINGERS

Guatemala

Jabel Tinamit Spanish School (2014, 2015, 2018)
Panajachel, Guatemala
A Maya owned and managed business, the school teaches Spanish and Kaqchikel to international travelers and local residents. Several teachers taught me songs across three visits.

María Carmelina Ajcalón
El gatito, 110
El patio de mi casa (1), 45
Juguemos en el bosque, 50
La vaca lechera, 122
La pequeña araña, 120
Periquito, 137
Que llueva, 58
Señor Lobo, 87
Un amigo, 145
Un elefante, 146

Nicolosa Peréz
La mané, 118
Los pollitos, 132
Pin Pon, 138
Pollos y pollitos, 57

Nicolasa, Florinda, and Carmelina
Campanita de oro, 42

Nicolasa, and Carmelina
Pin Pon, 138

Ingrid
El pato, 80
Cucú, cucú cantaba la rana, 103

María Carmelina Ajcalón (2020)
Buena Vista, Guatemala
Recorded in her home town, Carmelina shared songs in the Mayan language, Kakchiquel.

Jun Ti Sanik, 150
Ni Tz'unun, 152
Ri Utzil Iwach, 153

Escuela Modelo Inclusiva de Educación (2015, 2018)
Panajachel, Guatemala
A school for children ages four through eight, I observed teachers and children engaging in songs and singing games in 2015 while the school was in a temporary location on *Calle Santander* because their school was undergoing renovations. When I returned for subsequent observations in 2018, the construction project was completed and the faculty, staff, and students were relocated back to its original building on *Callejón el Capulín*. The children attend school either in the morning or afternoon and each session maintains its own faculty and staff.

Damaris Marely Mogollon Tecun de Santizo
Corre, conejito, 102
Doña Cigüeña, 106
El pato, 80
Las calaveras, 125
Pin Pon, 138
Un elefante, 146

Merlyn Rubí Celada García
El patio de mi casa, 45
La rana, 121
Muchos pececitos, 82

Luz Adriana Cutillo Mogollón
El caracolito, 44
Soy una serpiente, 67

Emma Leticia Chávez
Debajo de un botón, 105

Marí
Había un sapo, 114

La Familia González (2014)
Panajachel, Guatemala
We lived with the González family for one month in July 2014 during our first trip to Guatemala. They had three children, ages 10, 5, and 1. The father worked at a printing shop in Sololá and the mother took care of the children.

Ronda el campanario, 62
Vamos a remar, 148
Campanero, 99

Index: Sources: Sites and Singers

La Familia Ical (2015)
Panajachel, Guatemala
We lived with the Ical family for one month in July 2015. They had three children ages 17, 15 and 7. The father was a construction worker and the mother ran a used clothing store in the front of their house.

El toro toronjil, 49
El gallo pinto, 109
El pájara sin juala, 79
Ronda de la mano, 60

Nicaragua
Escuela Pablo Antonio Cuadra (2015)
Granada, Nicaragua
This elementary school for grades 1-6 is located in northern Granada and named after Pablo Antonio Cuadra (1912-2002), a famous Nicaraguan poet, playwright, and graphic artist. The children attend school either in the morning or afternoon and each session maintains its own faculty and staff.

A pares y nones, 41
Bate, bate chocolate, 72
Buenos días, 95
Cabeza, cara, hombros, pies, 98
Chocolate, 74
¿Cuántos años tiene la niña? 75
Doña Ana, 43
El barco se hunde, 77
Había un sapo, 114
Hazlo conmigo, 115
Periquito el bandolero, 83
Pikachú, 84
Tengo una casita, 144
Tierra y mar, 89
Va a preparar una ensalada, 91

Escuela La Amistad (2015)
Masaya, Nicaragua
A two-room public preschool where Isabel teaches 25 neighborhood children ages 4, 5, and 6.

Buenos días, mi maestra, 97
Caracol, 101
Doña Ana, 43
El baile de la gallina, 76
El árbol de la montaña, 107
En el lejano bosque, 111
La lechuza, 117
La pequeña araña, 120

La vaca Lola, 123
Los patitos, 130
Mi burro, 134
¿Quién se comió el pastel? 85
Salí, tortuga, 66
Sol, solecito, 141
Tierra y mar, 89

La Mariposa Spanish School (2015, 2017)
San Juan de La Concepción, Nicaragua
A Spanish school for international travelers, the visitors study, volunteer, and engage in a variety of activities to explore and learn about Nicaragua. I learned songs from many teachers at the school.

Asalia, Luis, Marcala, Tamar, Marelya, Milder, Maivin, Heydi, Claudia, Clavelioi, Paleska, Brandon, Dariela, and Guillermina
Abuelita de Perú, 71
Doña Ana, 43
El patio de mi casa (2), 47
La pájara pinta (2), 53
Nerón, Nerón, 55
Que llueva, 58
Rueda, rueda, 64
Soy una serpiente, 67
Soy una taza, 142
Su, su, su, 88
Un elefante (2), 147

Asalia Janeth Mercado Moraga
Familia Dedo, 113
Tortillitas, 90
Yo me gozo, 149

Lidia Hernandéz
Gallina colorada, 81
Sana, sana, 86

Anonymous
El florón, 78
Salta, mi conejito, 140

Nora Blass Hernández (2015)
San Juan de La Concepción, Nicaragua
Lidia, one of my teachers from La Mariposa Spanish School, brought me to her house to visit her mother, a retired elementary school teacher who sang many songs in her classroom. We enjoyed a sunny afternoon together filled with music.

Index: Sources: Sites and Singers

Buenos días, mi maestra, 97
Canto de las vocales, 100
De colores, 104
La hormiguita, 116
La lechuza, 117
La vaquita, 124
Las manitos, 127
Las verduras, 128
Salió la gallina, 139

Children at Escuela República de Cuba (2015)
San Juan de la Concepción, Nicaragua
A public elementary school for grades 1 through 4.
Buenos días, 95
Caracol (poem), 73
Los pajaritos, 129
Sol solecito, 141
Un elefante (2), 147

Dariela and Children (2017)
San Juan de la Concepción, Nicaragua
Sponsored by La Mariposa Spanish School, this preschool was held in Dariela's house. The children ranged in ages from four to eight years old.
Había un sapo, 114
Marinero, 133
Soy una taza, 142

La Familia Paéz (2015)
Granada, Nicaragua
I studied Spanish with the mother, Johanna, at her house. She and her daughter shared a few singing games with me.
Doña Ana, 43
Que llueva, 58
Rueda, rueda, 64

Sarahí (2015)
Granada, Nicaragua
Sarahí was one of my Spanish teachers and she shared a few songs with me.
Estrellita, 112
Panadero, 136

INDEX: SUBJECT

Animals
Canto de las vocales, 100
Caracol, 101
Caracol (poem), 73
Corre, conejito, 102
Cucú, cucú, cantaba la rana, 103
Debajo de un botón, 105
Doña Cigüeña, 106
El árbol de la montaña, 107
El baile de la gallina, 76
El caracolito, 44
El gallo pinto, 109
El gatito, 110
El pájaro sin jaula, 79
El pato, 80
El toro toronjil, 49
En el lejano bosque, 111
Gallina colorada, 81
Había un sapo, 114
Jun Ti Sanik, 150
La hormiguita, 116
La lechuza, 117
La pájara pinta (1), 51
La pequeña araña, 120
La rana, 121
La vaca lechera, 122
La vaca Lola, 123
La vaquita, 124
Las verduras, 128
Los pajaritos, 129
Los patitos, 130
Los pollitos, 132
Mi burro, 134
Muchos pececitos, 82
Ni Tz'unun, 152
Periquito, 137
Periquito el bandolero, 83
Pollos y pollitos, 57
Salí, tortuga, 66
Salió la gallina, 139
Salta, mi conejito, 140
Sana, sana, 86
Señor Lobo, 87
Un amigo, 145
Un elefante (1), 146
Un elefante (2), 147

Body
Buenos días, 95
Cabeza, cara, hombros, pies, 98
Hazlo conmigo, 115
La mané, 118
Las calaveras, 125
Las manitos, 127
Ronda de la mano, 60

Classroom
La lechuza, 117

Colors
Buenos días, 95

Counting and Numbers
A pares y nones, 41
Abuelita de Perú, 71
Bate, bate chocolate, 72
¿Cuántos años tiene la niña? 75
El barco se hunde, 77
Gallina colorada, 81
Las calaveras, 125
Un elefante (1), 146
Un elefante (2), 147

Family
Abuelita de Perú, 71
Campanita de oro, 42
¿Cuántos años tiene la niña? 75
Familia Dedo, 113
¿Quién se comió el pastel? 85

Food
Bate, bate chocolate, 72
Chocolate, 74
Las verduras, 128
Tortillitas, 90
Va a preparar una ensalada, 91

Friendship and Love
La pájara pinta (1), 51
La pájara pinta (2), 53
Un amigo, 145

Greetings
Buenos días, 95
Buenos días, mi maestra, 97
Ri Utzil Iwach, 153

Index: Subject

Health
Sana, sana, 86

Home
El patio de mi casa (1), 45
El patio de mi casa (2), 47
Soy una taza, 142
Tengo una casita, 144
Rueda, rueda, 64

Lullabies
El gallo pinto, 109
Caracol, 101

Nature
Caracol, 101
De colores, 104
Doña Ana, 43
El árbol de la
   montaña, 107
El florón, 78
En el lejano bosque, 111
Estrellita, 112

La pequeña araña, 120
Que llueva, 58
Sol, solecito, 141
Tierra y mar, 89

Occupations
Campanero, 99
Marinero, 133
Mi burro, 134
Panadero, 136

Religious
Corre, conejito, 102
Había un sapo, 114
Yo me gozo, 149

Town
Campanero, 99
Nerón, Nerón, 55
Ronda el campanario, 62

Transportation
El barco se hunde, 77
Vamos a remar, 148

INDEX: SONG TYPE

Additive
El árbol de la montaña, 107
Mi burro, 134
Periquito, 137

Kaqchikel Language
Jun Ti Sanik, 150
Ni Tz'unun, 152
Ri Utzil Iwach, 153

Poem
Caracol, 73

Rounds
Buenos días, 95
Campanero, 99
En el lejano bosque, 111
El gallo pinto, 109
La lechuza, 117
Panadero, 136
Ri Utzil Iwach, 153
Vamos a remar, 148

Spanish Language Variants
Buenos días (Frère Jacques), 95
Campanero (Frère Jacques), 99
El gallo pinto (Let's Put the Rooster in the Stew), 109
En el lejano bosque (One Bright and Sunny Morning), 111
Estrellita (Twinkle, Twinkle Little Star), 112
La lechuza (Frère Jacques), 117
La pequeña raña (Itsy Bitsy Spider), 120
Marinero (A Sailor Went to Sea, Sea, Sea), 133
Panadero (Frère Jacques), 136
Ri Utzil Iwach (Frère Jacques), 153
Vamos a remar (Row, Row, Row Your Boat), 148

INDEX: GAME AND MOVEMENT TYPE

Chains (additive)
Soy una serpiente, 67

Chains and Captives
Campanita de oro, 42
Nerón, Nerón, 55
Pollos y pollitos, 57

Chasing and Running
Abuelita de Perú, 71
Doña Ana, 43
El pájaro sin jaula, 79
El toro toronjil, 49
Juguemos en el bosque, 50
Muchos pececitos, 82
Señor Lobo, 87

Dance
Ronda el campanario, 62

Elimination
A pares y nones, 41
Abuelita de Perú, 71
El barco se hunde, 77
Gallina colorada, 81
La pájara pinta (1), 51
Muchos pececitos, 82
Periquito el bandolero, 83
Que llueva, 58
Rueda, rueda, 64
Salí, tortuga, 66
Tierra y mar, 89

Fingerplay
Familia Dedo, 113

Guessing
El florón, 79

Handclapping
Chocolate, 74
Pikachú, 84

Su, su, su, 88
Tortillitas, 90

Jumproping
¿Cuántos años tiene la niña? 75
Va a preparar una ensalada, 91

Movement: Responsive
Cabeza, cara, hombros, pies, 98
Caracol (poem), 73
Corre, conejito, 102
Cucú, cucú, cantaba la rana, 103
Debajo de un botón, 105
Doña Cigüeña, 106
El baile de la gallina, 76
El patio de mi casa (1), 45
El patio de mi casa (2), 47
El pato, 80
Había un sapo, 114
La mané, 118
La pequeña araña, 120
La vaca Lola, 123
Los patitos, 130
Periquito, 137
Pin Pon, 138
Ronda de la mano, 60
Soy una taza, 142
Tengo una casita, 144

Movement: Creative
Bate, bate chocolate, 72
Caracol, 101
Hazlo conmigo, 115
La hormiguita, 116
La mané, 118
Las calaveras, 125
Las manitos, 127
Los pajaritos, 129

Winding
El caracolito, 44

INDEX: FORMATION

If not listed, formation is free choice

Standing Circle
A pares y nones, 41
Abuelita de Perú, 71
Campanita de oro, 42
Doña Ana, 43
El barco se hunde, 77
El patio de mi casa (1), 45
El patio de mi casa (2), 47
El toro toronjil, 49
Juguemos en el bosque, 50
Los patitos, 130
Nerón, Nerón, 55
Periquito el bandolero, 83
Pollos y pollitos, 57
Que llueva, 58
Ronda de la mano, 60
Rueda, rueda, 64
Salí, tortuga, 66

Sitting circle
El florón, 78
¿Quién se comió el pastel? 85

Partners in concentric circles
Ronda el campanario, 62

Partners
Chocolate, 74
Pikachú, 84
Su, su, su, 88
Tortillitas, 90

Single line
El caracolito, 44
Los patitos, 130
Soy una serpiente, 67
Señor Lobo, 87
Tierra y mar, 89

Jumproping
¿Cuántos años tiene la niña? 75
Va a preparar una ensalada, 91

Groups of three, scattered
El pájaro sin jaula, 79

INDEX: NOTATIONAL LITERACY

Consider these literacy suggestions carefully and give priority to first embedding the songs into your curriculum as they have been in practice in communities for generations.

steady beat
Abuelita de Perú, 71
Bate, bate chocolate, 72
Chocolate, 74

♩ ♫
A pares y nones, 41
Bate, bate chocolate, 72
Chocolate, 74
Las manitos, 127
Los pajaritos, 129

𝄽
Buenos días*, 95
Estrellita, 112
Familia Dedo, 113

𝅘𝅥𝅯𝅘𝅥𝅯𝅘𝅥𝅯𝅘𝅥𝅯
El florón, 78
Las calaveras, 125
Pikachú, 84

♩
El gallo pinto, 109
El patio de mi casa (2), 47
Un elefante (2), 147

♪, *anacrusis*
Canto de las vocales, 100
El baile de la gallina, 76
En el lejano bosque, 111
Salí, tortuga, 66

♫ ♪
Hazlo conmigo, 115

♫
¿Cuántos años tiene la niña?, 75
Gallina colorada, 81
Las calaveras, 125
Tortillitas, 90
Va a preparar una ensalada 91

𝅘𝅥𝅯𝅘𝅥𝅯𝅘𝅥𝅯
Gallina colorada, 81
Periquito el bandolero, 83
Tortillitas, 90

♩. ♪
El patio de mi casa (1), 45
Un elefante (1), 146

𝅘𝅥𝅯𝅘𝅥𝅯
Debajo de un botón, 105
En el lejano bosque, 111
Un amigo, 145

♫♪
Sol, solecito, 141
Va a preparar una ensalada, 91

♫
El pato, 80
Rueda, rueda, 64

2/4
A pares y nones, 41
Chocolate, 74
Periquito, 137
Pollos y pollitos, 57
Que llueva, 58

4/4
Bate, bate chocolate 72
El gallo pinto 109
Hazlo conmigo 115
Los pajaritos 129
Los pollitos 132

3/4
Salta, mi conejito 140

6/8
De colores, 104
El caracolito, 44
La pájara pinta (1), 51
La pájara pinta (2), 53
Ronda de la mano, 60
Vamos a remar, 148

mixed meter
Rueda, rueda, 64
Va a preparar una ensalada, 91

Index: Notational Literacy

sol-mi
Las calaveras, 125
Sol, solecito, 141

la
Las manitos, 127
Pollos y pollitos, 57
Rueda, rueda, 64

do
A pares y nones, 41
Las manitos, 127

re
Hazlo conmigo, 115
Ronda de la mano, 60

sol_1
Buenos días*, 95
Canto de las vocales, 100
Doña Cigüeña, 106
El patio de mi casa, (1)
El patio de mi casa, (2)
La pájara pinta, (1)

la_1 sol_1
Soy una serpiente, 67

do^1
Cucú, cucú cantaba la rana, 103
El caracolito, 44
El gatito, 110
La pequeña araña, 120
Pin Pon, 138

fa
Buenos días*, 95
El toro toronjil, 49
Estrellita, 112
Los pajaritos, 129
Nerón, Nerón, 55
Que llueva, 58
Salta, mi conejito, 140
Un elefante (2), 147

ti_1
Cabeza, cara, hombros pies, 98
El gallo pinto, 109
En el lejano bosque, 111
La rana, 121
La vaca Lola, 123
La vaquita, 124
Las verduras, 128
Ronda de la mano, 60
Un amigo, 145

ti^1
Debajo de un botón, 105
Los pollitos, 132
Yo me gozo, 149

---

* Buenos días has four lyrical variants in this book: Panadero, La lechuza, Campanero, and Ri Utzil Iwach

INDEX: SPANISH LANGUAGE LEARNING

This index is intended for teachers (music, classroom, and Spanish language) to integrate Spanish language objectives.

Counting and Numbers
A pares y nones, 41
Abuelita de Perú, 71
Bate, bate chocolate, 72
¿Cuántos años tiene la niña? 75
El barco se hunde, 77
Gallina colorada, 81
Las calaveras, 125
Un elefante (1), 146
Un elefante (2), 147

Letters
El patio de mi casa (2), 47

Vowels
Canto de las vocales, 100

Time
Señor Lobo, 87

Opposites
Caracol (night/ day), 101
El baile de la gallina (in front/ behind), 76
Hazlo conmigo (fast/ slow), 115
Periquito (above/ below, in front/ behind), 137
Pikachú (up/ down), 84
Ronda de la mano (little/ big, tall/ short), 60

Vocabulary
Cabeza, cara, hombros, pies (body parts), 98
Corre, conejito (movement verbs), 102
El árbol de la montaña (parts of tree), 107
El pato (wing, foot, beak, tail), 80
Familia Dedo (family members), 113
La rana (animals), 121
La vaca Lola (head and tail), 123
Los pajaritos (animals, movement verbs), 129
Mi burro (body parts), 134
Soy una taza (kitchen items), 142
Tierra y mar (land and sea), 89
Va a preparar una ensalada (vegetables), 91
Yo me gozo (days of the week), 149

Ser y Estar
Buenos días (estar), 95
Buenos días, mi maestra (ser), 97
Campanero (estar), 99
Canto de las vocales (ser y estar), 100
Doña Ana (estar), 43
El florón (estar), 78
El patio de mi casa (1) (ser), 45
El patio de mi casa (2) (ser), 47
El toro toronil (estar), 49
Estrellita (estar), 112
Familia Dedo (estar), 113
Juguemos en el bosque (estar), 50
La vaca lechera (ser), 122
Las verduras (ser), 128
Pin Pon (ser), 138
Salta, mi conejito (estar), 140
Soy una serpiente (ser), 67
Soy una taza (ser), 142
Tengo una casita (ser), 144

Por y para
Buenos días, mi maestra (para), 97
Caracol (poem) (por), 73
Doña Cigüeña (por), 106
El baile de la gallina (por), 76
El florón (por), 78
La vaca lechera (para), 122
Los pajaritos (por), 129
Los patitos (por), 130
Ronda el campanario (por), 62
Salió la gallina (por), 139
Sol, solecito (por), 141
Soy una serpiente (por), 67
Tengo una casita (por), 144
Tortillitas (para), 90

Lyrical Improvisation
Doña Ana, 43
El toro toronjil, 49
Juguemos en el bosque, 50
Las manitos, 127
Los pajaritos, 129
Señor Lobo, 87
Soy una serpiente, 67
¿Quién se comió el pastel? 85

Index: Spanish Language Learning

Preterite Tense
El caracolito, 44
El gallo pinto, 109
El gatito, 110
La pequeña araña, 120
Muchos pececitos, 82
Periquito el bandolero, 83
¿Quién se comió el pastel? 85
Ronda de la mano, 60
Salí, tortúga, 66
Salió la gallina, 139
Salta, mi conejito, 140
Un amigo, 145

Imperfect Tense
Caracol (poem), 73
La pajara pinta (2), 53

Preterite and Imperfect Tenses
Cucú, cucú, cantaba la rana, 103
En el lejano bosque, 111
Había un sapo, 114
La hormiguita, 116
La rana, 121
Marinero, 133
Periquito el bandolero, 83
Un elefante (1), 146
Un elefante (2), 147

Future Tense
A pares y nones, 41

Campanita de oro, 42
El toro toronjil, 49
Estrellita, 112
Juguemos en el bosque, 50
La mané, 118
La parajara pinta (2), 53
La vaquita, 124
Sana, sana, 86
Salió la gallina, 139

Present Progressive
Doña Ana, 43
Juguemos en el bosque, 50

Ir + Infinitive
A pares y nones, 41
El patio de mi casa (1), 45
Pollos y pollitos, 57
Ronda de la mano, 60
Tengo una casita, 144
Va a preparar una ensalada, 91
Vamos a remar, 148

Subjunctive Tense
A pares y nones, 41
La mané, 118
Pollos y pollitos, 57

Commands
Buenos días, mi maestra 97
Caracol, 101
Hazlo conmigo, 115

INDEX: ALPHABETICAL

A pares y nones, 41
Abuelita de Perú, 71

Bate, bate chocolate, 72
Buenos días, 95
Buenos días, mi maestra, 97

Cabeza, cara, hombros, pies, 98
Campanero, 99
Campanita de oro, 42
Canto de las vocales, 100
Caracol, 101
Caracol (poem), 73
Chocolate, 74
Corre, conejito, 102
¿Cuántos años tiene la niña? 75
Cucú, cucú cantaba la rana, 103

De colores, 104
Debajo de un botón, 105
Doña Ana, 43
Doña Cigüeña, 106

El árbol de la montaña, 107
El baile de la gallina, 76
El barco se hunde, 77
El caracolito, 44
El florón, 78
El gallo pinto, 109
El gatito, 110
El pájaro sin jaula, 79
El patio de mi casa (1), 45
El patio de mi casa (2), 47
El pato, 80
El toro toronjil, 49
En el lejano bosque, 111
Estrellita, 112

Familia Dedo, 113

Gallina colorada, 81

Había un sapo, 114
Hazlo conmigo, 115

Juguemos en el bosque, 50
Jun Ti Sanik, 150

La hormiguita, 116
La lechuza, 117
La mané, 118
La pájara pinta (1), 51
La pájara pinta (2), 53
La pequeña araña, 120
La rana, 121
La vaca lechera, 122
La vaca Lola, 123
La vaquita, 124
Las calaveras, 125
Las manitos, 127
Las verduras, 128
Los pajaritos, 129
Los patitos, 130
Los pollitos, 132

Marinero, 133
Mi burro, 134
Muchos pececitos, 82

Nerón, Nerón, 55
Ni Tz'unun, 152

Panadero, 136
Periquito, 137
Periquito el bandolero, 83
Pikachú, 84
Pin Pon, 138
Pollos y pollitos, 57

Que llueva, 58
¿Quién se comió el pastel? 85

Ri Utzil Iwach, 153
Ronda de la mano, 60
Ronda el campanario, 62
Rueda, rueda, 64

Salí, tortuga, 66
Salió la gallina, 139
Salta, mi conejito, 140
Sana, sana, 86
Señor Lobo, 87
Sol, solecito, 141
Soy una serpiente, 67

Index: Alphabetical

Soy una taza, 142
Su, su, su, 88

Tengo una casita, 144
Tierra y mar, 89
Tortillitas, 90

Un amigo, 145

Un elefante (1), 146
Un elefante (2), 147

Va a preparar una
 ensalada, 91
Vamos a remar, 148

Yo me gozo, 149